Portraits of Recovery

Portraits of Recovery

Sixty Stories of Hope and Faith

Adam Gaynor

PENGUIN
STUDIO

To my grandfather Bert Shoeneman,

whose love and inspiration are with me every single day. I miss you.

———————————

PENGUIN STUDIO

Published by the Penguin Group

Penguin Books USA Inc., 375 Hudson Street, New York, New York 10014, U.S.A.

Penguin Books Ltd, 27 Wrights Lane, London W8 5TZ, England

Penguin Books Australia Ltd, Ringwood, Victoria, Australia

Penguin Books Canada Ltd, 10 Alcorn Avenue, Toronto, Ontario, Canada M4V 3B2

Penguin Books (N.Z.) Ltd, 182–190 Wairau Road, Auckland 10, New Zealand

Penguin Books Ltd, Registered Offices: Harmondsworth, Middlesex, England

First published in Penguin Studio 1997

1   3   5   7   9   10   8   6   4   2

Copyright © Adam Gaynor, 1997

Foreword copyright © Terence T. Gorski, 1997

All rights reserved

LIBRARY OF CONGRESS CATALOGING-IN-PUBLICATION DATA

Gaynor, Adam.

Portraits of recovery : sixty stories of hope and faith / Adam Gaynor.

p.   cm.

ISBN 0-14-026344-6

1. Recovering alcoholics—United States—Case studies. 2. Recovering addicts—United States—Case studies. I. Title.

HV5279.G39   1997

362.29'28'0973—dc20   96-38401

Printed in the United States of America

Set in Adobe Garamond

DESIGNED BY BRIAN MULLIGAN

Contents

Foreword   xi

Introduction   xiii

Bud   3

I think I used every possible excuse for drinking: if things went well, I drank heavily; if things didn't go well, I drank heavily.

Kat   5

And he knew that his little girl was a junkie. That was really shameful. I was so full of shame. When I saw him, I just immediately started weeping and I couldn't stop.

Derrick   7

I kicked and screamed, but if it wasn't for the fact that I wasn't able to walk out of detox freely, I would not be alive now. I know that for a fact.

Ed   9

We just got in a wreck. I was filled with a lot of compassion for the people that I had harmed. There was no reason for them to be hurt had I not been drinking and driving.

Tina   11

One night I got busted for the gun. The cop took me home, and I smoked up with my mom all night. I didn't feel anything when I was using. I really just didn't care. I wanted to be daring and live on the edge.

Darlene   13

I remember one day going to church and pulling up my sleeves and showing my arms to the minister and breaking down and crying.

Nancy and Dick   15

Sometimes it's hard being sober and having people die from this disease around you.
It is sad. But I do not have the power to stop some other person from using drugs or alcohol. This is an insidious disease and it's a deadly one.

Jack   19

I had a lot of fear of facing life on life's terms, and I knew it was always comfortable to have something to hide behind, so I went on methadone. I did methadone every day for eighteen years.

Billy   21

Alcoholism has taken a lot of family members and friends of mine. And I've always thought that I couldn't be one of those people, but I'm beginning to understand that I could very easily be one of those people.

Patty   23

"There's nothing left here but the dead and the dying." I said, "I'm going to Florida. I'm going to go live with my mother. I'm going to start a new life." And he wasn't ready, just like I wasn't when somebody told me.

Lee   25

Some of the things I saw, I just couldn't imagine why. So there was this hole that I was trying to fill up, and I tried some other things, but drugs were the only thing that filled that hole.

Amy — 27

I used to have dreams and keep them exactly an arm's length away just so I could always have them. I thought if I ever tried to go for them, I would either fail or find out that they weren't really what I wanted, and then I'd be crushed.

Guy — 29

Society sometimes places this label on me that because of my sexual behavior or because of my IV drug use, I got what I deserved. And that's not true, because no one deserves to die from diseases that are as brutal as these.

Sam — 31

I've learned through experience that I can't drink socially anymore. Still, it's not like being sober's a paradise or anything. You still have your problems, but you stick around and you work them out.

Sarah — 33

"Sarah, you don't remember what happened?" What does that tell you? I didn't really think about it. Go on with the rest of your life. Oh well.

Marianne — 35

Other times I thought I was really funny, sexy, smart, or cute, but I never really knew which I was going to be each day as I started drinking. I really didn't know who I was at all.

Jackie — 37

It is important that as a society—you know, human beings—that we must see how dangerous it is for us to use mind-altering substances, because it is hurting the human race as a whole. It really is.

Paul — 39

I would love to not have to think about the wreckage in my past. When I look back on the people I've met actively using and not using, it blows me away. It's two different lives. Through both, I've experienced a lot, so I know that I'm not missing anything.

Brian — 41

Something attracted me, though, to the nastiness of South Central. I loved the excitement, the drug environment. I felt fearless, like nobody could touch me. I lived in Watts, and that's where I learned cocaine.

Elena — 43

Then at the end of the day, there was nothing. I was completely devoid of any feeling. And I already had so much Valium in me, I would just pass out.

Joelene — 45

It was, and still sometimes is, so difficult to let go and not try to control everything, but I just can't see going back to where I was. That kind of escape just isn't an option anymore.

Bud and Eilish — 47

In my friendship with Eilish, I've allowed myself to get close to another person. Eilish is fun and busy, and she never sits and feels sorry for herself. She's always doing things for other people.
When I saw these young kids who had AIDS going into the hospital, I'd go into the hospital to see them. That's when I started knitting booties.

Kevin — 51

You soak a cucumber in a brine, it now chemically changes into a pickle. But you can never change that pickle back. Chemically, we're past the point where we can just have one drink. I've proved that to myself time and time and time again, doing the research.

Warner — 53

I remember after being clean for a week or two, looking out a window and seeing the sky. It was clear and bright in color. It reminded me of *The Wizard of Oz*. It was a moment of clarity for me. I knew then that all I had to do was stop using to get where I wanted to go.

Janel — 55

My sobriety is the most important thing in my life. It comes before everything. Anything I have now wouldn't be worth a damn if I wasn't sober. I'd lose everything.

Ralph   57
So for anybody reading this thing: If you're having a hard time, so am I. So is everybody. Somebody told me to not pray for an easy life but to pray for the strength and courage to find the thing, whatever it is, that fits you.

Jennifer   59
I was very lucky that I didn't get killed. And there were lots of instances where I could have been murdered. I used to think, "Dear God, don't let me get killed. Don't let me die."

Joel   61
My concept of addiction is not so much about the substance you use. It's about the whole personality. I was an addict long before I got high.

Susan   63
I've learned in this work and in my own life that if a person doesn't want it, there's nothing you can do to help them. Sometimes people are forced to change, but it doesn't last. It has to come from within.

Michael   65
The irony is that I got the most support from bikers in recovery—people who felt alienated because they were who they were.

Iris and Jimmy   67
I remember looking through the window of a jail and seeing Iris being locked up. I had a sense of loss, but the truth is, I realized that I didn't want to have to go out and get drugs on my own again.
I didn't go into treatment because I wanted to deal with being HIV-positive or because I wanted to stay alive. It wasn't about that. I went into treatment and tried to get clean because I was sick and tired of living like that.

Darlyn   71
When I was getting high, I believed that things would always be against me. I would always be pushing up against society, against my idea of success, against what I felt I needed to be in order to be a whole person, and I don't feel that way at all now.

Meg   73
Addicts have a tendency to deal with problems differently, and that's the biggest part of getting sober. We have to learn how to change. We have to change how we deal with things.

Mark   75
You're scared that emotions will destroy you, but you learn how to get through them and not be annihilated by them. You learn that you bounce back and you can handle a lot more than you think you can handle.

Mary   77
When I read the characteristics of an alcoholic or addict, I had those before I ever started using. I felt like an outsider, I felt different from other people, and it seemed like I felt things more strongly than other people.

Lee   79
So I went to treatment at the VA hospital. That's when I started to deal with these issues from the war and find out that it was okay to be a Vietnam veteran and be comfortable with yourself. I don't have to carry no shame or nothing or hide all these feelings.

Sandra   81
The drugs and alcohol made me forget, made me somebody I thought I wanted to be. When I see kids now that are ten, eleven, and twelve, like I was, it makes me sick that nobody was there to protect me.

Candacy   83
My sister was a biology major, and she was telling me things that I didn't know, like to lie on my stomach because it put the least amount of pressure on my heart, and to try to keep breathing. My mother was crying, "Oh my God, we're losing her."

Lowell   85
Why do they call it a disease? Because it's got a lot of the same symptoms: it's chronic, it gets worse and not better, and it has a set of predictable symptoms that lead to either insanity or death.

Lee 87

Because, first of all, they don't think that they have any problems except with the police. There's a lot of denial; none of them are convinced. They think their problems are legal and don't got to do with the drugs or alcohol that they're taking.

Kim 89

It's not just me anymore. If I mess up or am too drunk to see what's going on, look at what I could lose. I look at her and I see so much hope, so much that I didn't have.

Jude 91

I asked him if he loved me and he squeezed my hand, yeah. It hit me right then that I didn't hate him, that I was just like him. We were both drug addicts and alcoholics. We could only do what was in our natures.

George 93

I asked the heart specialist if a little drink would hurt me. "No it won't bother you." Three weeks later I was back at work and drinking heavily again. I couldn't stop.

Nancy 95

In early sobriety a lot of people think they're going to die, which is kind of funny. It's like they think that they won't be able to deal with the feelings they have.

L.W. 97

I learned a lot from my relapse. After it was over, I was liberated once again. I was shown at the deepest level of my being that I am an alcoholic and it is not going to go away. And it's much easier to lead a sober life than to try to change who I am.

Traci 99

Food abuse escalates just like drug addiction. Just as the drug and alcohol abuse got more and more severe, the food got more and more restricted, and the exercise got more and more intense.

Keith 101

There's an old line I heard from someone who had stayed sober successfully for several years. He said, "My mind is like a bad neighborhood; I should never go in there alone." You need help to get and stay sober.

Del 103

It was hard not using after they died, but both my friend and my lover died clean. And that is something I would like to do. I knew then that if I used, I would do it to die, not to get high.

Hoac 105

When the government took young people off the reservations and put them in boarding schools or foster homes, they were taken away from their teachings and traditions. So they don't have any values to say why something is good or bad.

Stevie 107

I thought, I'll never fly again. But when I got clean, I was given wings. That's when I really began to live a life that I could hold on to with both hands.

Andrew 109

You're having a crisis in your life and I know just how to solve it. But if it involves romance or finance, I am a helpless little salmon thrashing around in the banks of the street while this big bear is coming down on me.

Cecilia 111

And then after a while, you would tend to get complacent and you would think, "Well, I haven't picked up in a long time, and all these people just have the same old things to say and they're getting really boring." And that's such a dangerous time, because you get bored.

Hal 113

I have this beautiful home, I have this business, money, all this materialistic stuff, and yet I'm miserable.

Kathy   115

But since I've been in sobriety, all they do is look at me in wonder and say, "We don't know who this person is." Sometimes I don't know either, but that's the real Kathy, that's the real me who has been hiding for so long.

Michelle   117

I turned around and walked right off that roof. I had never been in such a bad state before. But I knew at that point that I was done; that was it. That's why I stopped using; it wasn't any fun anymore. It just wasn't working.

Del   119

Being in recovery as long as I have, you have to keep finding new tools and reinvent yourself and keep growing. As long as you are sober, you have to keep finding new ways.

Jim   121

My recovery has nothing to do with finding new places to be a man. It has to do with the integrity of people and my work with relationships.

Yvette   123

Then my father came downstairs to ask if I was okay, and I was so embarrassed. I could see the disappointment in his eyes. But I still wanted him to go away so I could finish smoking.

Rollandrock   125

I let the kids know that there's a loneliness to be found in a bottle that can't be explained. It's the kind of loneliness that is accompanied by thoughts of suicide and total desperation.

Jennifer   127

There was a mirror in the hallway I had to pass on my way out to the backyard, and I remember feeling very scared after looking in it because my face had become so gray.

Acknowledgments   128

Foreword

CHEMICAL DEPENDENCY IS A FATAL DISEASE. But this simple fact wasn't made real to me until I met a patient named Alex.

Alex was lying on his back with hoses coming from his nose and arms. He was an alcoholic and he was dying. He had been totally abstinent from alcohol and drugs for more than three months. He wanted to recover, but for Alex it was too late. His drinking had destroyed his liver. His alcoholism would kill him in spite of his newfound sobriety.

Alex wasn't bitter. He was grateful that he had his last few months of sobriety. "Being sober lets me face my death with dignity and peace," he told me. "I want my death to mean something, so I asked my doctor if I could talk to some people who work with alcoholics. I just want to share my experience. Maybe my story can convince others to get help before it's too late."

He wanted me to know that if he had it to do over again, he would never have started drinking. "My father died of alcoholism," Alex said. "But he was a real drunk. He couldn't keep a job. He abandoned both my mother and me. I only saw him when he came to ask my mother for money."

Alex made a commitment when he was ten years old that he would never be like his dad. And he never was. Alex worked every day of his life, right up until he collapsed at work, jaundiced and feverish from the liver disease that was caused by his alcoholism.

Alex had always supported his wife and two children. He earned a good living. He worked every day. He was a good husband and dad when he was home. "I didn't believe that some-one like me could be an alcoholic," Alex said. "Sure I drank heavily, but I thought I was handling it, and so did most other people."

Alex had never met an alcoholic. He had never been told that alcoholism was a disease. All that mattered to Alex was that he wasn't a drunk like his dad. He felt deep in his soul that alcoholism happened only to moral degenerates and skid row bums. That no responsible person would let it happen to him or her.

"Maybe if I had met someone like me it would have changed my mind." His voice was getting weak and he was straining to keep talking, but he wanted to go on. "I'm young. I'm only in my forties. I've lived a good life. I drank too much, but I worked every day. I supported my family. I got promoted. I contributed to the community. I even went to the scouts with my son. And now I'll be dead and there's nothing I can do about it. Maybe if I had met someone like me I would have seen the truth. Maybe if I had met someone like me I would have gotten in recovery sooner, before my alcoholism gave me the death sentence."

Alex closed his eyes and fell into a fitful sleep. I wish I could say that there was a peaceful look on his face, but there wasn't. He was dying in agony from a treatable disease.

I remember walking out of the room, stunned. "Alex is just a regular guy," I thought. Alex was a lot like me. He reminded me of my neighbors and friends. He was the kind of guy that I could have modeled myself after.

Yet, he was dying. He had the best medical care, paid for by his company's insurance plan. His wife, children, and parents visited him every day. And yet, alcoholism had killed him. And what's even worse is that he never knew he was sick until it was too late. Why? Because he had the mistaken belief that "Regular guys like me can't die of addiction!"

As I am reading *Portraits of Recovery*, I keep seeing Alex's face. I keep hearing his words. I also see the faces of many other people like Alex—people who died because they were just normal people who believed they couldn't get addicted to alcohol and drugs.

As I page through the brief stories and the photographs, I see pictures of real people in different walks of life who are suffering from addiction. In many ways all of these people are like Alex. But there is one vital difference. These people have learned about their disease. They know that it can happen to normal and ordinary people. They saw the warning signs and they got treatment early. Often, those who loved them had seen their disease and forced them to look at reality and get help.

Chemical dependency is a nondiscriminatory killer. It attacks people of all races, professions, and economic groups. It attacks people who have the dreams, desires, and lifestyle preferences that we all share.

The stories in *Portraits of Recovery* showed me these real people, the disease that threatened their lives, and what they did to get into recovery. But it was their pictures that stood out to me the most. It was their pictures that confronted me with a critical reality—chemical dependency is a disease that can attack anyone.

I couldn't help but think that, perhaps, if Alex had been given this book five or ten years earlier, he might be alive today.

As you read this book, pay special attention to the pictures. Look deeply into the eyes of these ordinary people. They are sharing their stories with you, as Alex did with me. Perhaps because of their sharing others may live.

As you look into their eyes and read their stories, look into yourself. Think about those that you love. Are you or someone you love sick with a fatal disease? Are you failing to see that disease because you mistakenly believe that "Ordinary responsible people like us can't get addicted"?

To recover we must have the courage to face ourselves in the minds and hearts of others. *Portraits of Recovery* gives each of us that opportunity. It moved me in a very profound and powerful way. This book could become the gift of life for anyone who takes the time to page through it.

—TERENCE T. GORSKI
President,
The CENAPS Corporation
September 1996

Introduction

A LARGE PART OF MY OWN RECOVERY has been getting to know others who are sober and sharing our experiences. A significant part of the recovery process is to remind yourself where addiction has taken you, and more important, what you can achieve in sobriety. I created *Portraits of Recovery* in the hope of inspiring those struggling with alcohol and drug addiction to take positive action for themselves. The loneliest and most frightening part of my own addiction was that I was unaware that help was available to me and sobriety was possible.

THE PEOPLE portrayed in this book have abstained from alcohol and drugs for a minimum of one year. I thank and applaud them for their courage in stepping forward to help others by sharing themselves and their stories. It is this kind of devotion and spirit that supports and sustains the recovery community. These testimonials are designed to inspire those who may be coping with drug and alcohol addiction by showing the many manifestations of the disease in people's lives and the near-miraculous effects of choosing a sober lifestyle.

THE WRITTEN accounts that are presented here are the by-product of interviews with each subject. These interviews were transcribed and distilled in order to provide as cohesive a story as possible. All of the testimonials reflect true-life experiences that illustrate the wide-reaching effects of the disease. Drug and alcohol addiction is blind to social and economic background, and can affect anyone.

I GREW up in an affluent suburb of New York where I spent every day of my teenage years getting high. At the time it seemed that the drugs made me feel better about myself. Yet, as my disease progressed, I found myself in burned-out buildings on the Lower East Side of Manhattan. There I maintained my high. There I bought drugs, stepping over the stoned bodies of junkie friends, totally oblivious to anything but my mission. Sick and in the grip of my addiction, I was committing a slow suicide and I didn't even know it. My eyes opened when I learned that a casual acquaintance had gotten clean. For the first time there was a glimmer of hope: if she could do it, maybe I could too. I asked for help.

WHEN I look back on my own journey into recovery, I'm amazed at the remarkable changes that have occurred in such a short span of time. The transformation I have undergone since moving away from active addiction to a clean and sober life has inspired me to document this same journey of others in this book.

IT'S IMPORTANT to realize that the power to cope with addiction resides within us all, and that utilizing this power is the first step to personal freedom. The book you now hold in your hands will, I hope, offer a glimpse of this.

—ADAM GAYNOR

Portraits of Recovery

Bud

IT WAS THE SO-CALLED THREE-MARTINI LUNCH ERA. It was very common for businessmen to go out and have two or three martinis for lunch with a couple of stingers afterward before going back to work. A lot of business was done over lunch, just as it was over golf or meetings. Working for a large corporation I found this was very common. There was always heavy drinking going on.

IT GOT to the point where not only was I drinking at lunch, I was drinking practically every night. After work I would stop and have several drinks, usually martinis. After I left the bar, which I never left until closing, I'd come home and mix a couple more. Usually I was late for dinner, and it created a lot of problems, as you can probably imagine. I think I used every possible excuse for drinking: if things went well, I drank heavily; if things didn't go well, I drank heavily. If I was having problems with people at work, I drank heavily. It started to affect my mood. I rationalized everything I did, blaming other people for my personal problems. Drinking made a big difference in my life, enough to get me in a lot of trouble.

I GOT three DWIs over a ten-year period. The third one was the worst because I had to go through the legal process and the city workhouse. It was a pretty horrible place to be, because the people that were in charge there were pretty bad. Fortunately, I was in during the Huber Law, and I could go to work during the day. That helped. But each time I came back from work I was strip-searched—going from a suit and tie to being entirely stripped, having a guard check to see if I was carrying drugs. It was pretty humiliating. That in itself was bad, the treatment there was bad, and the people in there were bad. It was not only for people with DWIs, it was for child abusers and rapists.

WHILE IN the workhouse I looked back on my life a lot. I looked back at a lot of the things I had done, a lot of the things I was trying not to do. I looked at my future. I think I was ready to accept some things in my life that I wouldn't accept before. I decided to try to straighten myself out. I knew that I enjoyed drinking immensely. I did have a lot of fun drinking during my life, but it had gotten me into a lot of trouble, embarrassment, and guilt. I think having that time to think about it was important. I accepted a lot of things in my life as an individual that I would not accept before. I had a hard time talking about my feelings and sensitivities. I consider myself a very sensitive person. A lot of people think I'm very cold, but I'm actually very feeling. One of my problems is that I'm a perfectionist, so I want everything to be just right. I would like myself to be the perfect individual, but that's not the way my life is and neither is anybody else's.

I AM retired now. I have a lot more time than I used to, but I haven't been bored. If you get bored, you tend to slip back into old ways. I have kept busy working on my house and painting. That keeps my mind active, instead of sitting in front of the TV and thinking, "Oh, hell, I think I'll get drunk."

Kat

I WAS LYING ON THE PLASTIC COT IN THE JAIL, starting to wake up, thinking I'm still in my bed at home in Wisconsin and this didn't happen. I was wishing it was true, that I was still at home and that I wasn't busted again. But I woke up and realized where I was and all the shit had really happened. That's when I really felt it, I think that was my turning point. My father lived in New Jersey at the time, so he came and bailed me out of jail. And he knew that his little girl was a junkie. That was really shameful. I was so full of shame. When I saw him, I just immediately started weeping and I couldn't stop. I love my father and I had let him down, you know. That's the way I felt. He was just like, "It's okay. Come on, I'm going to take you home." But I could see the pain in his face over knowing this.

MY AUNT was also there. They brought me back home and sat me down at the table and talked to me. My father had gone through treatment three years before and my aunt worked at a detox unit of a hospital. Those two sat me down and talked to me. They asked me questions, then said, "Why don't you try going into treatment?" They offered this to me and I said, "Yeah, I want to do it." That was the point where I surrendered, I guess. Between being in jail and seeing my father and having them offer this to me . . . I'm so lucky that they both knew what addiction was and what to do about it. So my aunt pulled strings for me and she got me into this detox, and from that minute on, I think I made a pretty deep surrender. This is my first time in recovery. This is my first time clean, and I didn't have to relapse after that.

THERE'S BEEN times where I felt more pain than I thought I could deal with. I've been in so much emotional pain that I thought it would kill me, but it hasn't. I mean, just maybe a month shy of my one-year anniversary, my father died, but I didn't have to pick up over it. That's really cool, but there's still some pain left in that spot that I haven't dealt with. But I've got that feeling now of energy and of playfulness and centeredness and serenity and calmness that I always got from my drugs before. I've got that for myself. And just being in a place of so much pain and then being able to reach out to people, regardless of what they are going to say or think, because I've gotten to a place of trusting—that is really beautiful.

Derrick

YOU CANNOT JUSTIFY ME and my history with a one-word answer, but there is no mystery in that. I try to keep things in perspective. Regardless of everything, Derrick is sober. Derrick has one day at a time done something he never thought he could do. And a higher power, if you will, has done for me what I could not do for myself. Now there is more or less a deep gratitude and a thrill about existence and life. When you come close to being dead and come to know years and years of not believing that you can live for even twenty-four hours without chemicals, and can come to be productive, that is excitement. Life is never dull to me; it is a constant thrill. So that's what sobriety is for me. It's like, look what I've done. A couple of months ago, I had a dream that I was writing a book. Honest to God, and the name of the book was "Miracle," because that is a word by which I perceive what my life is. It's like something that you see, a fantasy. You have this guy in the gutter, picked up by the police—vomit, jail, soup line, slime, menace to society, violent. And when I look at my life now, it's nothing but a miracle. I guess I must think about that a lot, to have a dream that I wrote a book called "Miracle." It's fantastic and that's an understatement.

ONE THING that I'll probably never forget: I was dying in a hospital. What had happened—I was at a local park. There was still snow on the ground, it was toward the end of the winter season. I passed out face-down in the snow after drinking a bottle of gin. Not a lot of people come through the park at night when it's wintertime. Some passerby, I still don't know who it was, called the paramedics. The paramedics got me to the local hospital. I was dying from hypothermia. My body temperature was down to the point where the doctors did not know if they could pull my body temperature back up. My father called from Chicago, saying, "Derrick, shouldn't this be enough?" And I said, "Yes!" Really believing that I'd almost met my maker, this should be enough. Lo and behold, after I came out of the hospital, I had set up a companion to come to the hospital and bring a fifth of gin. I walked out of the hospital drunk. I took my last drink on the night of April 4, 1986, and that's very vivid because I fell into the Mississippi River. I was in a park on Nicollet Island in Minneapolis. I was drinking with a drinking companion. It was gin, I remember it was gin. The next thing I knew, I was in the river. I don't really remember much about that night. I was evidently dragged out by this companion. The police found me on Fourth Street in Minneapolis, in a bus shelter. And to be quite honest and humble, with no pants on, according to the report. I was very drunk! The police put me into detox for about the twentieth time, and a chronic counselor at the detox made a decision about me. She did what is called a commitment, because I always came into detox hurt, scraped up, having seizures, and a lot of physical things happening. They kept me in there under judge's rule because they thought I was going to kill somebody or kill myself. So I was forced to go into my last treatment, and it was my blessing in disguise. I kicked and screamed, but if it wasn't for the fact that I wasn't able to walk out of detox freely, I would not be alive now. I know that for a fact.

Ed

EVEN THOUGH THERE WASN'T ALCOHOL and drug abuse in my family, there was a lot of the same insanity and dysfunction that goes on in an alcoholic home. I clammed up. I grew up walking on eggshells. I didn't know it was okay to feel the feelings that I had. I was constantly being compared to my older brother by my mom. At least that was my interpretation. I never had my own identity. Why couldn't I be as good in school as my older brother? Why didn't I excel in sports like my older brother?

THERE WERE different ways of escaping or not dealing with the difficulties I was having in my life at those times. I just could not fit in. I always felt like an outcast, and I didn't feel that way with people who were getting high. That seemed to be the one common thread we had with each other. When I'd get high, I'd get to the point where I'd black out and not be conscious of what was going on. I guess that was the ultimate escape, the ultimate of not feeling anything. I was uninhibited. I felt like there wasn't a bunch of pressure on me. And I just got into tranquilizers real severely for a while, shooting them, selling them, writing scripts, or using blank scripts and having someone else fill them out.

THEN CAME the DUIs, and I caused real injuries to some people. My drinking was affecting innocent people. I had a problem. I had a lot of guilt, shame, grief, and remorse. I damned near killed three people in my last car accident. Innocent people, people I didn't know. We just got in a wreck. I was filled with a lot of compassion for the people that I had harmed. There was no reason for them to be hurt had I not been drinking and driving. I think that's what it took to really open my eyes that my problem was a little more severe than what I thought. I started to see the full reality and scope of my problem.

I WAS suicidal for about a month. A couple of mornings I woke up with this emotional bottom I was hitting. *I hope these people don't die from these injuries.* I was just obsessed in the mind with it, and there was no place to escape. I couldn't escape into the bottle. I couldn't escape into the drugs. I saw that making a geographical change wasn't going to get me out of the legal battles I was faced with, and I knew that if I ran, eventually my drinking would catch up to me again. You know what they say, wherever you go, that's where you are. Thank God that God had other plans and intervened. It was during this time that I ended up in treatment, and that's where I needed to be because I probably would have found some kind of way to do something that was life-defeating.

Tina

FIRST OF ALL, I was addicted at birth because my mom was using all the while she was pregnant with me. And until I was nine years old, she gave me drugs to keep me quiet, so I wouldn't cry, so she wouldn't hear me cry.

I WAS in foster homes, then with my dad. I drank his alcohol, then moved back with my mother when I was fourteen. She and I started using together. I used heroin with her and cocaine. I started getting involved with gangs. I started getting more violent, carrying a gun, stealing, and fighting. One night I got busted for the gun. The cop took me home, and I smoked up with my mom all night. I didn't feel anything when I was using. I really just didn't care. I wanted to be daring and live on the edge.

I FEEL sad when I look back, but life sober is great. I know who I am now. I make better decisions for myself and know how to find healthy places for me. I'm learning; I like learning. Getting my education is important to me. No one in my family ever graduated from high school. I'm going to be the first. I know I've had a messed-up life—and so did they—but I'm getting over it. They're just sitting there. They don't deal with it and I do.

I CARE about people, but there are some people I just had to give up, like my mom. She's not good for me, so I had to give her up. I gave up my best using-friend. My family and some of my old friends aren't happy that I got sober. They're jealous. I have what they want but won't choose to get.

MY LONG-TERM goals are to help the homeless and to help kids who are abused, who are taken out of their homes because of the abuse. They need someone to talk to who relates, not just someone who got into the field and learned about it in college. I know firsthand, so I can give them honest advice. I also want to get married and adopt two little girls from Honduras. Two little girls I baby-sit are from Honduras. They're so cute and lovable.

I WORK harder than I did when I was using, but it isn't hard anymore to stay sober. It's what I want—no ifs, ands, or buts. I have hope now. I've learned over and over again to have hope. I don't get everything I want, but I'm happy. I was never happy. There are down times, but they go away. Happiness comes and it's worth it. Every minute of it.

Darlene

I DID NOT THINK IN TERMS OF GETTING SOBER because I had never heard the concept. It's not like I knew about recovery and I was just choosing not to do it. I had never heard of recovery. I was trying to treat my depression by doing drugs. I never even thought in terms of never doing drugs again. I just thought some people were able to live without drugs because that's just the way they were. Like my mother, she just didn't drink. And so I was trying to find my niche—going to church and working with kids. I remember one day going to church and pulling up my sleeves and showing my arms to the minister and breaking down and crying. This was before he was supposed to go out for a sermon, and they had to stall everything. He made some phone calls and found a treatment program that I went to that first night. I remember seeing some of the things that were written on the walls there and breaking down and crying because I knew that there was hope.

WHEN I first got clean, I had a Mercedes and a man that, even though I worked, paid all my bills. Suddenly I realized that I couldn't sleep with him without drugs. I knew that much. I remember talking to people about it. The responses that I got were like "Don't be no fool, don't use the drugs." I felt like say-ing, "You see that Mercedes? You see how that house is fur- nished?" But in my heart I knew that if I stayed with him, I'd get loaded. Certain things had to go at any cost. I was willing. I had to tell him, "I'm sorry, but I just can't do it anymore. If I do, I'm going to get loaded, and I'm going to die."

THE LONGER that I stay sober, the more lessons that I learn. One of the things that I have today, that I didn't have before, is a sense of myself. If you had asked me to name five things that I loved about myself, you would have had a lying woman on your hands, because there weren't five things that I could name. Today there are things about myself that I love and ad- mire. I have the confidence to say what my gifts are. As an African-American woman with a sense of herself, I'm aware that I have a powerful presence, which I can use to help oth- ers. For instance, I'm the case manager at a school here in San Francisco for women with low income. I bring a real motiva- tion to the job. In other programs, if you don't show up for class, nobody's gonna call you, nobody's going to tell you that you can do this. When I speak, I have the ability to articulate for other people what they think but are unable to express the way I do. My message is simple: You can overcome the odds.

Nancy and Dick

Nancy On September 29, 1975, Dick took me out to dinner. That was exactly two years from the date that we had met. I was leaving him. I had been married to an alcoholic before. So when they brought the bottle of wine, he took a sip of it and toasted me. He said, "This is the last drink I'm ever going to have." I just thought I was going to fall off the seat, because I'd heard that so often, you know, from men. My second husband used to do those kinds of things, and now he was telling me this. I said, "Yeah, sure, sure." But I felt that he was asking me for another chance for our relationship. So I started getting some help myself. I'd come home and he'd say, "What did you learn tonight?" And I'd say, "Pour me a drink and I'll tell you." And he dutifully would make me a bourbon. I'd sit down and tell him. I was so thrilled that he had quit drinking because it was so ugly, but I continued, moderately at first, but then it took over. And then I was scared. Scared because he was noticing the amount of drinking I was doing.

Dick I got sober first, but I was so codependent that I thought I could fix her. It was very painful to watch Nancy go down the tubes. And it was embarrassing at times; it was embarrassing for the kids. So we tried to cover up her drinking. But of course we didn't know the extent to which she drank. At the height of my codependency, I thought that, possibly, if I bought her some really good wines, some nice French wines, her favorites, and we sat in the living room at five o'clock, and

she had her couple of glasses of wine, that that would be much better than drinking rotgut. I was just so ignorant even though I was an alcoholic. See, I didn't know she was getting up not to go to the bathroom but to go to the basement and chug-a-lug a couple of glasses of cheap wine that she had stashed down there, or in the guest room or wherever. It was stashed all over the house. And the kids and I would always wonder, How could she be so drunk at the dinner table on two or three glasses of wine? God, she used to drink me under the table, and now she's a thimble. I didn't know she was doing three liters a night in the basement.

Nancy The fun today goes with the fact that Dick is my best friend. You have to know that for years I considered him my worst enemy. I say to him that I did not fall in love with him until after I got sober because, you know, there were so many circumstances—we were attracted by drinking together, we were doing things like that. And I think back to friends that I had in high school and the fun and things that I had with them, and that's exactly what Dick is now. He's a person that can have fun. He's been on this adventure of my education, since coming to Minnesota. I've studied to become a chemical-dependency counselor, and now I'm in graduate school for a master's in social work. I want to do private therapy with women that have chemical addiction problems—and other problems, like eating disorders, that type of thing. I just want

to give back. That's what sobriety has given me, the ability to give back. We have gone through some real sad things in the last ten years—we've both lost parents, we've detached from children with love—but it's because of a spirituality within that's guided us through. On the other side of it, nothing is as bad as it was when we were drinking.

Dick I think life is real simple. Nancy has this very interesting life with her education, and in 1989 I volunteered to become a housewife for a year—or homemaker, pardon me, I'm not married to the house. She keeps correcting me. It's such a joy for me to watch Nancy grow through her education. I do so-called women's work. Well, who says it's women's work? I'm a man, and I'm doing it. I don't make that connection at all. It's the simple things we enjoy, like walking down to get a smoothie or going to a movie. She always picks out tearjerkers. I'm a crier now. And that's okay. I'm emotionally bound up with people. I get a kick out of going to the store, shopping. I love to grocery shop. It's a kick. The biggest kick is watching the people. And, of course, there are the hundreds of friends we have around this country. It's amazing, just amazing.

Nancy Sometimes it's hard being sober and having people die from this disease around you. I've lost someone very, very dear to me. That was my second husband, who was the father of my daughter. He was a brilliant man. He died of alcoholism—excess fat on the liver. He just wasn't ready to get sober. He knew of all the other options. I had gotten sober. I had written him. I had let him know that I was here to help him if he ever wanted it. And that's the only thing today that I can do. Today I realize that I can't just pick anyone up and say, "I'm gonna get you sober." A person has to want to. You know, one of the things I'll never forget, that I heard when I was first sober, and I thought the woman who said it was very cold. We were talking about someone who had died from an esophageal hemorrhage, and I said, "How could God do this to a person? They were trying, they were really trying." And she looked at me and said something to the effect, "That was not God's will that that person died of an esophageal hemorrhage. That was self-will." And I came to find out that her son had died from a heroin overdose.

Dick It is sad. But I do not have the power to stop some other person from using drugs or alcohol. This is an insidious disease and it's a deadly one. People die. If you're an alcoholic without a strong spiritual basis, it's pretty hard to stay sober for life. Because at one time or another, alcohol will reach up and grab you. When I was eight and a half, nine years sober, Nancy couldn't stand me. And a friend, Kathy, said to me, "You were nicer, I liked you better when you were a drunk." And she's one of the people that said I should never have another drink. I remember saying to Nancy, "You know, I've been sober a long time now, it's been nine years or so. I think I ought to be able to have three or four glasses of wine." That's alcoholic thinking. It creeps in. Without a spiritual basis, alcoholics and drug addicts don't have a prayer.

Jack

I THINK AT THE TIME they didn't know much about it. Here in L.A., the methadone programs were fairly new, although they had been going on in New York for about ten years. I had been getting arrested and I couldn't kick the heroin, so the judge said I could either go to jail or go on the methadone maintenance program. I had a lot of fear of facing life on life's terms, and I knew it was always comfortable to have something to hide behind, so I went on methadone. I did methadone every day for eighteen years.

WHEN I originally got on the program, they said I would be able to go out and get a job and not worry about having to maintain my habit, but as it is with other drugs, doing methadone became a way of life. The program basically kept people medicated, and it helped the government keep track of where the addicts were, since you had to go in every day to get your methadone. Few people I met stopped using, they just switched to a legal drug. I've seen three generations of a family—grandmother, daughter, and grandchildren—all going to the methadone clinic every day to get their fix. It's not that uncommon.

I WAS an exception. Not many people who are on methadone for a long time ever get off it. One of the reasons is that detoxing from methadone is a nightmare, and it can take a year. I finally decided to get sober because as my daughter got older she started noticing how her mother and I used, even though we tried to keep it hidden. Our daughter said she didn't want to live with us anymore. I wasn't ready to let her go, so thinking like addicts think, I decided I'd put her mother in recovery—and she took off because she didn't want to stop using. So I had this daughter I was trying to raise alone, and I knew I couldn't keep using and take care of her. If there was one main reason for getting sober, it was my daughter.

I WAS also so physically sick that I couldn't even eat. My liver was going and I don't think I would have been alive much longer if I kept using. The methadone had so saturated my body that I had to be moved into the hospital to detox. It was a year before I had a regular night's sleep. To anyone out there who is on methadone, I say get off it now. No good can come of it. It only gets harder. I feel fortunate to have gotten off it. I have come to believe in miracles, divine intervention, whatever you want to call it. I don't know any other way to explain the changes I've been through.

MY RELATIONSHIPS with people, starting with my daughter, have gone beyond anything I thought possible now that I'm clean. I look back and see myself as just a hustling dope fiend who used people. But it's not that way anymore.

Billy

EVER SINCE I WAS A YOUNG BOY I had a pretty clear sense that I was an alcoholic. Both my parents were alcoholics, and although I was only eight years old, I already thought I was too much like them and believed I was probably like them in that characteristic too. Even as an adult I had no idea who I was. I mean, one day to the next I would try to define myself by what my job was—I was a stockbroker, I was a bond trader, or I was a good golfer. But I really had no sense of self, and no sense of self-worth for that matter. I wasn't a part of anything. I was this disconnected molecule. I totally lost the value of money, my money and other people's money; and regardless of how much money I had made, I would spend twice as much or three times as much and always try to live a grandiose life, thinking that I was doing such wonderful things and living in such wonderful places, having such intense experiences, therefore I must be okay. Geez, so many people don't get to do this. I must be all right. I mean, I'm like one percent of the population. Wow.

I WOULD go to work and I would look okay when I first got there, but then I would do a total meltdown because the eye-drops would no longer keep my eyes white. The two showers that I took before going to work didn't seem to keep me clean. Sleep deprivation always caught up with me. Often I would fall asleep and prop a tissue box up against the phones and crash in the middle of a trading day, when things are screaming and yelling around me. People would be pretty much hor-

rified, and I wouldn't give a shit. All I could think about was getting some sleep because I was so exhausted. I would work all day so I could get high all night, and I was always very fearful of losing my job because I wouldn't have something to define me. Plus I wouldn't be able to support my habit. I never realized that I actually had an interest in what I did until I was sober.

I THINK back about that time as Dr. Jekyll and Mr. Hyde. But I think I was a nice guy. I am a nice guy. I think people saw that. But in life there's more than being a nice guy—there's reciprocating, being part of a team and doing for others what they do for you. And I wasn't able to do that. I wasn't able to reciprocate anything. I was not very helpful or supportive, and I completely operated for myself. There are a lot of ugly memories. But it's not so much that I regret the past. Although I have a lot of amends to make and certain bridges to cross and crosses to bear as far as the wrongs that I've done, I think that helped me get to where I am today, which is sober. It's just the scariest thing that I've ever come up against. Alcoholism has taken a lot of family members and friends of mine. And I've always thought that I couldn't be one of those people, but I'm beginning to understand that I could very easily be one of those people. I don't want to be a homeless street person and I don't want to die and I don't want to kill somebody. I want to lead the life I'm living today, which is very full and a wonderful one.

Patty

LIFE IS OUTRAGEOUS, but there are gifts in sobriety. I left my husband in New York in 1987, and I told him, "I love you, but I gotta get clean. I'm forty-one years old, I've got no veins left. I got nothing. There's nothing left here but the dead and the dying." I said, "I'm going to Florida. I'm going to go live with my mother. I'm going to start a new life." And he wasn't ready, just like I wasn't when somebody told me. So I got in my car and I drove down to Florida, and I was real sick. I'd been shooting really strong synthetic heroin. I was coming off of methadone. I was drinking a lot of vodka, taking a lot of Valiums, but I didn't want to go into treatment because I know what it's like for opiate addicts in treatment. We don't sleep. You're in there with the crack heads, and they can't wait to fall asleep because they ain't slept in months. And you just sit there and look at the walls. I didn't do that. I went to live with my mother. I kicked at her kitchen table. I didn't sleep for a month and a half. It was real hard, but it was worthwhile.

ONCE I got clean, I knew that I wanted to work with addicts. I guess I caught some kind of save-the-world syndrome. This is how it started. Because of my behavior, I wanted to check myself out. I remember watching this movie where this actress was getting into a situation where she had some fear, and she said, "God, if you get me through this, I'll dedicate the rest of my life to helping these people." So when I finally went down for my HIV results, I did the same thing. I went into the bathroom, and I got on my knees, and I said, "Dear God, this is the big one. This is the one I can't handle. I'm willing to make a deal. If you see to it that I don't have HIV, then I'll dedicate the rest of my life to helping other addicts." And by the grace of God, my results were negative. So I went out and got myself a job working at a treatment center. I worked in West Palm Beach for three years. Now I'm working for the National Recovery Institute.

I FIND that working with other addicts is toxic. But when I'm not at work, I do things to replenish the supply of what I'm giving away. I do my meditation. I spend time with my spiritual adviser. I spend time with people in recovery. I do a lot of positive things for myself because work is very draining. I mean, you're sitting there listening to somebody's life story and people that have been sexually abused. What it does is it kicks up a lot of my own stuff. So I had to do a lot of work on myself before I could put myself in that position. But you know something that my spiritual adviser told me? She said, "You know, Patty, the darker the shadow, the brighter the light—and you spent so much time in the shadow, now it's time for you to come into the light."

Lee

WHEN I WAS USING, I saw myself as a symptom, a symptom of something that was much sicker than I was, which was a society view, the attitudes about substances, legal vs. illegal, alcohol vs. drugs, racism, etc. I grew up in Birmingham. The stuff I saw as a kid I didn't understand. And I still don't understand it today. Some of the things I saw, I just couldn't imagine why. So there was this hole that I was trying to fill up, and I tried some other things, but drugs were the only thing that filled that hole. They didn't make things go away, but it made it easier to deal with.

SO TO me, my addiction was a symptom of something much bigger, which is what I think we are seeing in the country today—child neglect. It doesn't mean that the parents have to be absent from the home for the child to be neglected. And it doesn't have to be anybody's fault. That's just how it happens. It's like, a kid relies on people to fill their needs and if they don't get them met, they figure out how to deal with the situation themselves. They make grown-up decisions as a child, so the addiction is a result of those decisions. I know I'm going on and on, but to me it gets deep sometimes when we talk about addiction and how we got here. "If you are going to do something, son, why don't you just drink beer." "If I ever see you smoking, I'll kill you. Bring me a cigarette." You know what I mean. A lot of that stuff. So it wasn't unusual for me to use.

I WENT through treatment six times, because I was smart. I was trying to apply logic to an illogical disease. Yeah, I was go-

ing to figure it out. So I kept going through treatment because that's what you do when you get to the end. This is the only door left. It's not that you are having this spiritual awakening. The bus to the VA hospital is just the only place to go. But it's almost as if I was supposed to go through that—especially when I look at what I do today, the type of work that I do. It's almost like I was paying some kind of dues or in some kind of school. People think I'm nuts for saying that, but I'm not saying it was some kind of prophecy for me to be born an addict, just that God used it as an opportunity to get me ready for something else.

I GET to talk for a living. What better job could you have, especially when you know what you are talking about. I get to travel all over the country to train people to start up street teams in other cities, because my friend and I, we pretty much developed this model that we use here in Atlanta. I'm also coordinating a project that's evaluating street-team outreach around the country, to see how effective they are in reducing people's risk of getting infected with HIV. I'm also an addiction counselor and I train other counselors. So it's like, I don't know what's going to happen next. I went to college, but I don't even have a degree. So for me to do the stuff that I get a chance to do, you know there is something unusual going on. There's no comparison to my life before, except to say that as bad as it got when it was bad, it's as good now. It's like the other end of the spectrum.

Amy

THIS IS THE CLOSEST I EVER GOT to spirituality. I was sixteen years old and I wound up overdosing in the bathroom of a club, face-first in a toilet, on alcohol and Valium. I ended up at the hospital, had my stomach pumped, the tubes through my nose and down my throat, the whole thing. And I woke up the next morning and looked around. There was this nurse sitting by the side of my bed and she just looked at me. She said, "You know, you should be dead. You really should be dead, because I saw what they pumped out of your stomach last night, and you really have no reason to be alive. God must really think you are special." And I was like, Huh? She gave me a Bible and she told me to really consider not hurting myself anymore because obviously God loved me and I was one of God's children, and that there was some kind of purpose that I had on this earth or else God wouldn't have sent me back. And I walked around with this Bible in my hand for a week. My mother was freaking out because we're Jewish and this was not the Jewish part of the Bible. I think it was mostly just the effects of coming off an overdose, that I was spaced out and I was like, "Oh, God loves me." I lost the Bible in my room somewhere and it just never came up again, and that was it.

I USED to have dreams and keep them exactly an arm's length away just so I could always have them. I thought if I ever tried to go for them, I would either fail or find out that they weren't really what I wanted, and then I'd be crushed. And being sober had given me the ability to try to go after these things, and some of them haven't been all that great. I would rather have kept them as fantasies. It's funny, because every time I find something that I think I really want, and I say, "Okay, I'm gonna go for it," and when it's not really as great as I wanted it to be, it only makes room for a new dream. You know, it's like I keep evolving and my dreams keep getting a little bigger, and I have friends who help me get them.

I WAS with someone recently and we were talking to some people about sobriety, so I told him about where I came from. My friend turned to me and he said, "I can't believe you drank at all. I can't believe that you really did all those things." And I said, "You see, people can change. Things can happen. I must be doing something right if you don't believe all that stuff about me, because it was all true. It really happened. I really did all those things and I really was a pathetic, lifeless person." I think that's where the hope comes in. It's like seeing someone who you respect and admire and knowing that they were once enslaved to their addiction. You see that change is possible and you can achieve a decent life through sobriety, and you can still be happy and have fun. It's so important. I like my life today. I wouldn't trade it. I wouldn't wanna be anybody else. I think that's the whole gift of it. Really just wanting to be who I am in this moment and being okay with it.

Guy

I'VE ALWAYS BEEN CREATIVE, even in my addiction. The difference is that in my addiction, I couldn't wait for the process to be complete. I rushed through everything, so that the end product was mediocre. Now it's like, I take pride in the whole process, from the first to the last stroke. And it's a part of me. I think the most enjoyment that I get is when I make really beautiful art. People recognize my ability to create it, and it feels good to be admired and to be desired.

WHEN I was younger, I had no idea what it's like to be HIV-positive, because you don't know what you have until it's taken away. I know that when I was out there using, I assumed and was usually right that most people were positive, but I would jones so hard. I would steal people's syringes after they had hit themselves up. There was still blood in the syringe and I would do it myself. That's a pretty frightening thing. It's great that I have all this caring now that I'm sober, but it would be really great if I didn't have to have all this caring. Right now I'm fighting two deadly diseases, but after a year of sobriety I've learned to distinguish between the two. I try really hard not to feel broken and less-than. I have to realize that I don't deserve either of these diseases. No one does.

Society sometimes places this label on me that because of my sexual behavior or because of my IV drug use, I got what I deserved. And that's not true, because no one deserves to die from diseases that are as brutal as these. It's strange, but being HIV-positive improves the quality of my life because I respect life a lot more. My time on this earth is limited, and you only get one chance at life. I can do it with drugs and fail or do it without drugs and be happy.

NOW I spend a lot of time on my recovery, trying to figure out who I am and where I left off. I work for an artist that's very successful, and because of the confidence I've built up, I have people working with me, trying to help me find my niche in life so that I can do my thing. I spend a lot of time with my friends who are in the same boat as I am, and I think that's my biggest support. I'm not going to die from the things that I'm going through, the feelings I've been putting away for so long. Life now is like a muscle inside my body that is full of the right things, and it's like a spark that I feed and it grows. It feels the same way that I feel when I fall in love: this tingling feeling that's warm and cozy and keeps me comfortable. That's all I know.

Sam

We had a nice home in Venice and my wife suddenly decided she wanted a divorce, and it really threw me. I started drinking, and it was getting worse and worse. So Consolidated Film Industries said they'd have to let me go because of the drinking, but if I stopped, they'd like to have me back. So I stayed out for about a year and was drinking heavily. Finally I called a friend and said, "Are there any jobs over there?" And he said, "No, but there's one at Universal Studios in the optical department." So I went out there, and I got the job. So things were just getting better. I tried to just drink socially, but into the fourth year I started to drink really heavily, and I started taking days off and they had to let me go. That's where I got my camera card. I got the show "Green Acres." And I stopped drinking to keep my job, but later into the years, I started drinking heavily again. Then I started freelancing here and there. All I cared about was making enough to pay my rent and my alcohol. You have to reach some kind of a bottom, like losing your jobs, but that was not my bottom. My bottom was one of the mind—going crazy.

You have two choices, death or insanity. There's nothing in between. Toward the end, it doesn't get to be any fun anymore. I remember at one point—I had been sober for seven months—I was going to go out and drink socially and handle it differently. Just having a few drinks lasted about three days, and then I got blasted. Once an alcoholic, always an alcoholic. I've learned through experience that I can't drink socially anymore. Still, it's not like being sober's a paradise or anything. You still have your problems, but you stick around and you work them out. I don't know. It was a big mess. Drinking is the source of so many disasters, not only for the person drinking but for the people around them. Staying sober is hard, but it gets easier. It takes one year before the desire passes. That's what kept me going out—the desires. But if you wait them out, they pass. And you get a little stronger each time you fight it.

One of the things that I struggle with is goals. When I retired, I didn't set any. But you take it a day at a time. Sometimes it gets lonesome. I do a lot of walking. Still, I've had some incredible things happen. One day, my neighbors asked, "When's the last time you saw your parents?" I said, "Oh, about thirty years ago in Flemington, New Jersey." So a few days later I'm walking by, and they called me in and gave me a ticket to New Jersey with $500 cash in it. So I went home, and I'm glad I did. But you know something, when I went back there, there was this coldness. My sisters barely talked to me and my mother was very distant. So I was kidding and I said to my mother, "You know, I think I'll stay another week." And she said, "No you're not." Remember, this is after thirty years, and I wasn't drinking anymore. They would barely talk to me. So I was glad to get out of there, and I don't call them anymore. I didn't like the way I was being treated. That was fifteen years ago. They can't seem to forgive me. I guess what I have to remember is that addiction is addiction and that nobody has all the answers.

Sarah

THESE GUY FRIENDS OF OURS CAME UP to where we were camping, and they brought all this alcohol and weed and acid and stuff, and they just got us all fucked up, and I ended up getting raped. I didn't know that I was on acid that night. I found out the next day. It was just kinda like it happened. I didn't realize I'd been raped until I sobered up. I started talking about that incident and my friends were like, "Sarah, you don't remember what happened?" What does that tell you? I didn't really think about it. Go on with the rest of your life. Oh well.

WHEN I was using, I didn't really care. Using made me feel just kinda like I was free. I could do whatever I wanted. But I didn't—it was like—what's the word? I was just living. That's all there was to it. I was just staring at the corner. At the time I don't think that it really made a difference. I mean the person that I am now is like somebody that people would look up to. Before, it was like—I was just the party person, you know? "We'll go to Sarah's. Sarah will always get fucked up." That's all I would do. That's who I was. At the time, I thought that it was cool to be that person. And everybody was like, "Oh, Sarah will never quit. Sarah will always be doing it."

I GUESS I realized I had a problem when the cops showed up at my house. I didn't even believe it then. When I was in treatment, I believed it. A friend was over and we were getting drunk. I had a really high tolerance, and she is, like, a lot smaller than me and had a lower tolerance, but I was making her drinks the same as my drinks, and she got really drunk; and her parents came and picked her up, and they thought she was high. Her mom called the cops. And so they were watching us and watching the house, and then they thought I was dealing because there were always people coming over and leaving all hours of the night. And I wasn't dealing. And one day I was just sitting out in the garage talking on the phone and smoking a cigarette, and the cops came knocking on the door, and I was like, "Oh, hi."

I THOUGHT that was typical teenage life. But I missed out on doing a lot. When I was a little girl I always thought, When I'm in junior high school and high school, I want to be a cheerleader. I'm going to do this, and I'm going to do that. And I didn't do any of it. I didn't have the motivation to do it. One of the biggest things that I've heard from kids that are using is that they're, like, If I stop, I won't have any friends. I'll be alone. Or I won't have any fun. That's the biggest thing, that I won't have any fun. But I think that I have more fun now that I'm sober, because I can go out and do what I did before the drugs and remember it the next day. Now I do stuff like collect dolls. I like collecting dolls. I don't know what they do for me, but it's like being a kid again. Sometimes it's hard looking back at my past, but not really. That was who I was at the time. That made me who I am now. I'm not ashamed of it.

Marianne

I USED TO LOOK AT OTHER DRINKERS who were having problems and think, "Oh, that poor person"—while I was having a martini. And I wasn't just having one. I was having three. Before dinner. In these huge brandy snifters, so it was really like six. I was surrounded by family and friends who drank a lot, and I wasn't drinking as much as they were, so I thought nothing was wrong with me. I also didn't show it very much when I was drunk, although all my feelings were magnified by my drinking. Sometimes I'd get sloppy and start crying. Other times I thought I was really funny, sexy, smart, or cute, but I never really knew which I was going to be each day as I started drinking. I really didn't know who I was at all.

I WAS a daily drinker. But I thought it was all proper and the way sophisticated people lived, with the wine, martinis, and scotch. I basically drank by myself, and I think that's one of the things that made me stop. I tried going to a recovery group for a while, but it didn't do much for me. The first person I heard speak there was this guy who lived on the street, and he didn't have much to say to me. I went three times and thought I was cured. While I was going to this group I was still drinking, which I thought was in poor taste. I was really lonely. I could be in a crowd of people and still be lonely. Whenever I was in a crowd I thought there was something wrong with me

and everybody knew it, so I built this barbed-wire fence around me, and that fence stayed up for a while even after I sobered up.

I'VE BEEN sober ten years now, but my friends tell me that six years was a real turning point. I started to feel more comfortable in my own skin and trusted myself more. I stopped trying to impress people. I would bend like a pretzel to please anyone. I had always felt inferior but acted superior. I was trying to run the world, you know. And it took some time to get my ego down to a manageable size. Now I've decided that what other people think of me is none of my business. I don't have to bend like a pretzel for anyone.

I CAN look back with sober eyes now and see how everything has brought me to where I am. Some time ago I had given up on religion. I still don't care for the patriarchal religion I knew as a child. I have had trouble thinking in terms of a personal god. In the abstract I could conceive of some unifying energy, but I didn't see it giving energy to me. It just seemed too vast. Then my friend gave me a tape of this minister who said, "God is in you, not as a button is in a glass of water but as the ocean is in a wave." I liked that. I could buy it. So from that my belief has evolved. And now I have finally stopped running the world, which is a big relief.

Jackie

TO ME, ONE OF THE GIFTS is just knowing that it's okay that I have this disease and that there is a solution. To me, I think that's the greatest gift that I have. I know that whatever is ailing me, it's all right. There are other people that have this thing and there is a solution. Spiritually, I think that now the things that I appreciate are the things that you can't buy. At one time in my life I know that I was really possessed by material things. I had a lot of them. I had a call-girl business in New York. You know, me and the girls would sit around, get our minds wrecked, and we would have business. There'd be drinking and using taking place, all kinds of sex and money, and basically that was my life. I thought my life was a very good life because I was into big money and a lot of drugs. A lot of drugs. Spiritually, I did feel empty and really confused. I knew I wanted something that I didn't have, and even though I tried to maintain principles, there was a lot of shame and guilt about some of my behavior.

AFTER A while I went back to school and I got a degree in secretarial procedures. I thought my life would straighten up and I could get a good job in an office, and my life would change. It didn't. I found myself sitting at my desk, and when my boss was gone, I would put the coke on the desk with a straw and do lines. I'd go, "How can this be?" I'm, like, totally away from the negative environment and I end up doing the same things even though I'm in a professional setting. The thing that really blew my mind the most was, like, whenever I got my paycheck, I could spend the whole thing within a weekend, and that was for a whole month. I'd

be sad that following Monday because I didn't have gas to get to work. I would just wonder how I could continue.

I'M NOT willing to risk my life anymore. I'm not willing to risk my sobriety. I'm not willing to risk my spiritual being that I've accomplished, that I've been enlightened to—my spiritual condition. I don't want to do anything that will harm that, and I know sometimes chasing after material things, sometimes your spirituality takes a backseat. I've had that happen in my recovery the first time around. So today I'm learning that all the things I've wanted and needed, they will materialize. And if they don't, then that's okay too. Today I want to be a beautiful person inside. Of course the outside is important too. I wanna look attractive and be a pleasant person to be around, but for me the thing that I am aspiring for is to become spiritually correct, and that means the beauty from within. And you can't do it using any mind-altering substances. I'm convinced of that. That's the true advantage for me.

I HOPE that there is a message in what I am saying, that I can make a difference in the world. It is important that as a society—you know, human beings—that we must see how dangerous it is for us to use mind-altering substances, because it is hurting the human race as a whole. It really is. I hope that I can encourage someone, anyone, to find a power that's greater than themselves and live life, accept life, as it is. You can be happy without anything from outside. You can be happy just as you are.

Paul

I NEVER THOUGHT THAT I'D BE WHERE I AM TODAY. I certainly never thought that I'd be in Minnesota, married to a wonderful woman. I never pictured the jobs that I've had here. I've always had this grandiose vision of myself as the benevolent dictator of the world. So far, that position hasn't become available. I never, in my wildest dreams, thought that I would be opening a small ceramics shop in Minneapolis. It's too bizarre to believe. I told some of my old friends, and they were like, "What? What are you doing?" I'm excited about it, I'm also scared and overwhelmed. But I never pictured myself being as happy as I am. I'm just happy and normal, like everybody else. Well, not like everybody else. That's not true. I don't know how to describe it.

AM I upset that I have this disease? Yes and no. This disease has given me a life. Without it, I don't think that I would have done any of the things that I've done over the last few years. What I'm talking about is regretting it and not regretting it. The part that I'm not mad about is that it had given me the opportunity to live a life different than I ever expected, but full of promise and hope and interest and excitement and despair. Being able to deal with all those has made me more of a whole person. But I'm mad at it also. I would love to go out with my wife, Liz, who is a normal drinker, and just have a glass of wine, and I would love to not have to think about the wreckage in my past. When I look back on the people I've met actively using and not using, it blows me away. It's two different lives. Through both, I've experienced a lot, so I know that I'm not missing anything.

THERE ARE so many bizarre, sad, funny stories from when I was using. I was supposed to get married, and I guess that she knew that I wasn't in the best of shape, so I agreed to speak to a counselor a few days before we were supposed to get married. I missed the first appointment, and I came up with some stupid excuse that I'd hit a delivery boy with my car at 6:00 A.M. in New York. I don't know if she believed me, but she chose not to question it. In Philadelphia, I checked into some little hotel and smoked crack for the next three days, including the day that I was supposed to get married. Not calling anyone. People were supposed to be flying in—friends, family. I just disappeared. That was horrible.

SOMETIMES, NOW, when I tell stories with people that I know are sober, we just laugh and laugh, and it's absurd because it's not a laughing matter. I can laugh about it because I know what they're going through, because I've had similar experiences. But there's also a lot of shame. I was paralyzed as soon as I'd started using cocaine. Toward the end, I'd get paranoid and think that people were coming through the air-conditioning ducts and the TV. It's just pathetic and crazy. I'd end up in these places with people that I didn't know, with guns and shit and crazy stuff all around. And then I'd get up and go to my job and pretend that I was this big-deal real-estate person. That's all it was about: smoking cocaine, going out and doing weird things, and living on the dark side—because that's what attracted me.

Brian

THE LAST TIME I LIVED WITH MY MOTHER I had a tug of war with her over a pistol. The cops came by, so I threw my gun over the gate by my house. Later, I'm in the backyard making all this noise because I'm so high. And my mom comes out of the house, sees me picking up my gun, and tells me to give it to her. Now it's eight years later and she opens the yellow pages to show her friends the ad for my business, and she sometimes brings them over to my office so she can brag. I used to hate her, wish that she would get hit by a car. Now we're making plans together for my kid's birthday party next week. And I had a chance to go to Utah with her, where I showed her how to snowboard. Being able to give to my friends and family is the best part of my recovery.

SOMETHING ATTRACTED me, though, to the nastiness of South Central. I loved the excitement, the drug environment. I felt fearless, like nobody could touch me. I lived in Watts, and that's where I learned cocaine. I had a little taste of cocaine one time and it was, like, I need that stuff, where do I get it? I hung out with this pack of dudes, and our mission was to find rocks in Watts. We sold it and a lot of weed. After being sentenced for some legal problems, I came to the realization that I didn't want to do that anymore. I didn't want the jewelry, the money; and I didn't want to be a jerk anymore. A lot of people got fucked up because of my stuff. I ruined people's lives. I used to threaten people's kids when I was selling drugs. Then when I got out of jail I did some hard thinking and decided I had been taking life pretty relaxed. That was probably my first real commitment—to stop selling and start leading a good life. I knew that part of my commitment meant caring for people I didn't like, which was hard because I was a pretty mean fucker.

I LOST short-term memory, a lot of it is dead. And I remember losing it while smoking weed, and thinking, there it goes, going bye-bye, I'm getting foggy. I've gotten some back, but not all of it. I'm doing okay, though. I'm a Macintosh computer consultant. I do memory upgrades, work with software. I sit down with people who have a hard time with computers and teach them how to get along.

I LOVE computers and working with my hands, but I knew I needed to find a way to relieve my spirit, to let myself go. Since then, surfing has been spiritual for me. It was from the first time I tried it. You're floating out there on the water; you don't always know what's going on around you. You've got to watch all around you all the time. I've been stuck in riptides and nearly drowned, but I feel like a sea creature out there, like I'm part of the sea.

Elena

I OWNED A PSYCHIATRIC CLINIC that specialized in dependencies and addictions. I ran the clinic for about a year on Valium—I was blacked out half the time I was there. Someone would come into work on a Monday morning and say, "I'm here to work." And I'd say, "Who are you?" And he'd say, "You hired me on Friday." So it was crazy. I would send secretaries to take lunch breaks at 10:30 to get rid of them so my drugstore could deliver my Valium to the clinic. I was a figurehead, more or less. I would go to work and lock myself in my office. I was up to 300 milligrams a day and blacked out half the time I was there. It was very, very bizarre.

I ENDED up quitting my job, and I moved into the Chelsea Hotel. I think it was a suicidal thing. I know people who have gone there to die; they've overdosed. And of course, Sid Vicious was there. It was a great place to die. I thought I would be in my element. I could do what I wanted, and I could be as stoned as I wanted. Moving into the Chelsea was also a punishment. Basically, I had always been surrounded by tremendous luxury. I was out of my environment and the comfort of how I was living before. I could have gone to the Waldorf-Astoria, but I wanted to be in an element where what I was doing was acceptable.

EMOTIONALLY I was dead, I was entirely dead. I mean, just every once in a while I'd have a flash. I'd look in the mirror and say, "My God, you're not sober anymore." They were seconds—not even, split seconds—of reality. "What have I done? Ten years, I just blew it all." And then the only thing I could do to alleviate the pain was to just eat more Valium. I would be overwhelmed, so with a handful of Valium it would all be over.

IMMEDIATELY UPON waking were the times when I would have these flashes where I was devastated. That's why the first thing I always did was have my Valium and Perrier water all set up right next to the bed. I wouldn't get out of bed without taking it. Then I would dress, leave, and actually have to go to a hairstylist to have my hair washed and braided. I was incapable of doing it myself. I was too lethargic. Then I would wander around the Village, see some films or go to art shows, meet people for lunch. And it was very, very disturbing. I just had no direction. I had the option to do anything I wanted to do.

THEN AT the end of the day, there was nothing. I was completely devoid of any feeling. And I already had so much Valium in me, I would just pass out.

Joelene

THE HARDEST PART FOR ME was losing the fear, so I ran. That's what my using was about. I ran from my feelings, my own shadow, everyone and everything. I see now that my fear was a lack of faith, but replacing my fear with faith—with a belief that everything is going to be okay—was one of the hardest things I've ever had to do. I think I'd kill myself before I'd get loaded again. It was, and still sometimes is, so difficult to let go and not try to control everything, but I just can't see going back to where I was. That kind of escape just isn't an option anymore.

I'M GLAD I got sober when I did. I don't know if I would have been able to make a decision to get clean if I'd used any longer. Or if I would have even lived much longer. My parents first put me into treatment when I was twelve. I was living on the streets and they put me in, in part, so I'd have a place to stay. I stayed clean for about a year and a half, but I didn't want to be clean. I enjoyed what drugs did for me. When I was fourteen I stopped for good. I've been sober eight years last Monday.

THE DRUGS and the alcohol aged me by so many years. Getting clean gave me a chance to be my age again, but it was never the same. I don't think I have the same thoughts as other people my age even now. Being in recovery has brought me to some understandings that a lot of people my age don't have—like finding a higher power, admitting on a daily basis that I don't have control over everything in my life. When I first got sober and started going to a recovery group, I heard a lot of "I spilled more than you ever drank" from some older members of the group. Then I realized that it wasn't how long or how much I used but the reasons why I used and continued to use. Like I said, I got high to escape. Like when my brother died, my use skyrocketed. I was incapable of dealing with the pain. I had friends who said, "Let's go get fucked up. That'll make it all go away." But it didn't work. When you sober up, the pain is still there.

NOW I have friends who are a safe haven. If I call at three in the morning because my mind is running, they'll be there for me. I know every single morning I get up, I have somewhere to go where people will understand and maybe offer me something I need to learn. I work with teenagers now who are like I was, and I try to give them a safe haven. The recovery rate among kids isn't very high. I try to teach them a better way, but some of them don't want to believe me. They might die as a direct result of their drug use, which makes me want to shake them and say, "Believe me. It gets better. The pain goes away."

Bud and Eilish

Eilish You know I'm eighty-four. That's a ripe old age. I don't have a friend that I met since I came to America that's still alive. They're all gone! From age! When I went into recovery, I had trouble. I was drinking. She had a house that was a mansion and her husband's a doctor. She has these children and she asked me to come in and help her. What I didn't know was that she was one of those *pupils*, people who like to go to school all the time. All the time! The only time she was home, she was doing homework, doing more school! She had four children, five by the time I left there. I was with her eighteen years. And that's when I started drinking, because I felt like I was being used. I was taking care of her five children and she had a woman come in twice a week to do the floors in this twenty-five-room house. And I did the rest of it and got drunk every night on the Canadian Club.

I'M NOT afraid anymore. The only thing that I'm worried about is that I die sober. And it'll be twenty years on the second of November, so I'm not going to worry about it. If I can make twenty years, I can finish the rest of my life. That's the most important thing.

Bud Eilish and I met in 1976. I started going to Fred's recovery group. It was all gay men, but Fred asked Eilish to come to the group because if a woman was there it would be a little more respectable. Eilish had a recovery group at St. Patrick's Church. She asked me to come and speak on a Monday night

there. So I went, and it was filled with all these old Irish men and women. I was the first up-front queer that had talked there. What I did was simply tell my story, what my drinking was like, and what it was like to be sober. Basically, when I was fifteen I was hospitalized. I told my folks that I was gay, and I went to a psychiatrist. I knew that I was gay, that was not the issue. The standard treatment for homosexuality back in Minnesota in 1960 was shock treatment, so they gave me a series of shock treatments, and they fried enough brain cells to really disrupt my life. I left that experience with a lot of anger—although I wasn't aware that I was angry—and a lot of fried brain cells. But I was still gay. So they failed. Anyway, for the next fifteen years I drank and did drugs and was angry and resentful and afraid and unable to accomplish much of anything because I had real problems with my memory. I went to college a number of times and flunked out. I couldn't test because I couldn't remember. Then I finally got into recovery, and I quit drinking, and I quit using drugs. That was in 1976.

Eilish Bud was one of the first people that ever spoke for me at St. Patrick's. We had all the Irish people coming down. I accused them of coming down to pick up a little bit of the brogue and not just to get well. Then Bud got up and told his story. And you'd look at the women and they'd be crying. There'd be big tears coming out of their eyes. They were so shocked at what Bud had told them. They had no idea that people could suffer like that. I kind of thought that he was kind of an angel. I thought he was such a good man, to have such a sense of humor through everything. That was twenty years ago. And I still feel the same way about him.

Bud One of the things that happened to me in recovery is that I started being up-front about being gay. As I told my story at St. Patrick's, I remember the looks on people's faces, and I realized that I had things to be angry about. Over the last twenty years, one of the things that I have had to work on is my anger and my forgiveness. Because to the extent that I am willing to forgive what happened to me, I am able to take responsibility for my actions. It has been really difficult being responsible. What's my responsibility, what's not my responsibility? Dealing with anger and finding the willingness to forgive. I learned that I am responsible for what I say and what I do. What's done is done, what's over is over. What happened yesterday is gone, and tomorrow isn't here yet. I think that's what I learned in the program, that is what I have today. Then the job is, How do I make today as good as I can? And find people like Eilish to share my life with?

Eilish Bud accepts me, he's a friend. Everybody needs friends, but people in recovery and people who are sick and dying need them more. All my native people are gone; they're dead. I don't have a single friend that I met since I came to America that's still alive. My children have their own things to do. They're busy and they don't want to be bothered with me.

I can call Bud up anytime I wish. And if I think I'd like to do something, like go to the museum or dancing, I can call him.

Bud Eilish has a wonderful sense of humor and a way of looking at life that is very healing. At Fred's, Eilish would be in the midst of all these handsome gay men, having a wonderful time and knitting. That was very attractive to me, because with all the drinking and drug use I had done, I was very depressed. Eilish is a person who enjoys life, has fun, tells stories, and makes laughter. That's what I was drawn to. We do things together. We were on a retreat last summer and we went into town to this disco. We stayed there until two o'clock in the morning. Well, Eilish is over eighty years old. We told her children and they got a little upset, but they'll get over it.

IN MY friendship with Eilish, I've allowed myself to get close to another person. Eilish is fun and busy, and she never sits and feels sorry for herself. She's always doing things for other people. What I've gotten from her is the understanding that what I get out of life comes from what I'm willing to do for others. Eilish has given me a role model of how to live a life looking out for other people, because that's what she does. In the early 1980s, people started getting sick with AIDS. And Eilish would start knitting these little booties. Anybody that had been sick for a year, Eilish would knit them slippers. She became very famous. Then people started

dying. Of the three or four hundred people that have been to Fred's meeting, there are five or six of us left.

Eilish When I saw these young kids who had AIDS going into the hospital, I'd go into the hospital to see them. That's when I started knitting booties. The first man that we ever had with AIDS was Ryan. At that time, I was so horrified when I went to the San Francisco Hospital. He'd get into bed and he'd move the bed all over the room, the pain was so bad. And they'd try tying the bed down and putting in screws and so forth, and nothing stopped it. They didn't get to that place where they could stop the pain in the body. Every time I went over there, there was somebody in pain. When the lady I was taking care of died, I decided that I'd do something with San Francisco Hospital with the AIDS clinic, and I went out there to work. I offered to come in. I would get to work at eight o'clock in the morning and leave at about four or five o'clock in the afternoon. I really enjoyed doing that. Somebody told me I was the best volunteer they ever had.

Bud What Eilish says about me is what I would say about her. We have a good time together. In recovery, part of the trick is letting go of yesterday, not worrying about tomorrow, and celebrating today. When Eilish and I are together, we don't worry about yesterday, we certainly don't worry about tomorrow, and we have a wonderful time today. I think you have to have fun with somebody. I'm a loner and I spend a lot of time doing things by myself, but recovery is something that is shared with other people. All these people around us have died, and Eilish and I are left. We've survived so far.

Kevin

PEOPLE CAN BE INTELLIGENT and able to reason and make choices and choose, and not be able to stop that one thing that is destroying you. I've got a lot of respect for that now. I never used to give the devil his due, but I've heard the disease of addiction personified as the devil—as powerful, as animated. I have respect for that now, and I don't want to fight with active addiction anymore. I'm sure I'm still very active in the behaviors, but I have an opportunity to work on those, not being cluttered with the active part of the disease. I'm very aware that all I did was blow all my standards; it didn't matter if I was lying around with no clothes or no shoes or no money. The degradation aspect: You just accept shit that you wouldn't normally accept for yourself—to the point of sleeping in gutters, like the typical wino or junkie stereotype; to the point of death, you accept death as part of the game. Which I did. I accepted it. But when it came down to it, I was scared to die like that.

I LOOK now, and I still feel like it was a terrible, terrible love affair with alcohol. I had a feel for addiction, a totally co-dependent love affair. I mean, I loved alcohol with such a passion, it was uncontrollable. I haven't done enough work to find out why. I mean people say, "Oh, you have this and that, and you are medicating and you didn't want to feel." And I'm like, "I'm the kid who had everything, why would I want to shut down like that?" I think it was part of my nature. I tried it, I liked it, I pushed it past the point. The best way it was ever explained to me was an analogy where we're all cucumbers. You soak a cucumber in a brine, it now chemically changes into a pickle. But you can never change that pickle back. Chemically, we're past the point where we can just have one drink. I've proved that to myself time and time and time again, doing the research. I am grateful that I stopped doing it, and that I got the opportunity, although I don't understand why I got the opportunity. I've given God all the thanks in the world for that moment when I stopped. Because I tried at different times and it didn't work. The physical compulsion and the mental compulsion were always there. I didn't understand it; it was just easier giving in to it. My mind would think everything through, having an intellectual mindfuck, and I didn't come up with any answers. I just kept doing it.

WHEN I was using, I always said I didn't have a chance. Not many people who used drugs had a chance to get it and keep it. Whatever it was they wanted in life, they'd lose it, even their dreams. Now I've got a chance no matter what. I think I've developed something. I've believed in myself no matter what I was going through. So many people didn't. They look down upon a drug user or drug abuser, addict. I tried never to listen to that, because I believed that I had a little problem, and once it went away, I'd be all right. But it turns out the problem is me, and now I get a chance to work on these things.

Warner

ONE OF THE REASONS I FIRST STARTED getting high was because it intensified colors for me. Like the sky became really blue. But by the end of my using days, everything was dull and gray. I remember after being clean for a week or two, looking out a window and seeing the sky. It was clear and bright in color. It reminded me of *The Wizard of Oz*. It was a moment of clarity for me. I knew then that all I had to do was stop using to get where I wanted to go.

ANOTHER MOMENT of clarity came when I realized that I wasn't playing music anymore. My drug use stripped me of my relationships, my family, my music. Music had always been important to me. I remember looking at my guitar and it seemed to be crying, telling me it needed me.

WORK WAS always there, though. One of the things that kept me denying my problem was that I would go to work no matter what. As long as I had a job and wasn't sleeping in the gutter, I thought everything was okay. The insanity of it—I was a security guard for a department store—was that I would bust shoplifters, turn them over to the police in one room and then do a drug deal or do a line of coke in the next room. It was so bad.

FINALLY A friend took me to the hospital after I had done at least an eight ball of coke on my own. They sent me up to rehab, and the lady there started talking to me and could relate to me right away. I went home and was supposed to return the next day. But I wanted to use my last stuff before I went in. Then the lady from the rehab called me, and it was like she was reading my mind. She said, "I know what you want to do. You want to go and get your last high." So she called my bluff and I surrendered. I went in right away and haven't done any dope since. My favorite quote about that time of my life is that I was trying to use a chemical solution for a spiritual problem.

I USED to meditate a lot while I was doing acid, and it was often a really bad experience. I suffered from such paranoia. When I got clean, I was afraid to meditate. It's weird, though, how my higher power leads me to things. If I don't take the straight route to them, He'll still land me there eventually. I started having anxiety attacks when I was clean. They were so intense that I couldn't take the subway because I would have to get off at each stop and go above the street just to get some air. I went to therapy for it and learned again how to meditate—without acid. I haven't had any anxiety attacks since.

Janel

THE FIRST TIME I DID CRYSTAL METH, my favorite drug, I was with a guy named Spider. He was this big dealer or something, and I was twelve. I used it intravenously. It was fun. It gave me, like, the best feeling. I had energy and I was happy. I felt as if I could walk up to anybody—even if they were seven feet tall and 500 pounds—and say anything I wanted. It made me so brave. I remember running through the mall naked, screaming, "We are all naked in the eyes of God!" I don't know why I did that, but that was crystal meth. Made me do crazy shit.

BUT NONE of it was truly fun, and I wasn't truly happy. In fact, life sucked. I overdosed a lot. The last time I used, I overdosed. I didn't even know my own name. I kept saying the name of my boyfriend at the time. I thought I was him, I guess. I finally saw through the bullshit, though. I realized that nobody really cared about me. I overdosed, was nearly dead, and all these people who I thought were my best friends in the world were laughing. None of them cared enough to help. By the time the paramedics got there, I wasn't breathing. That was the last time I saw any of my old friends. But that's all right.

THESE BIG cuts on my arms are from my last treatment. I was coming down off everything and started to remember past abuse and felt really shameful. The only way I could get away from the pain was to cut my arms. It actually felt good. It's really sick, I know, but it was the only way I could deal, since I couldn't really talk about it. One night I was all alone, so I was going to kill myself. I was walking down the road and stood up with my feet on the rail of this bridge. I was ready to jump—I don't see why I didn't fall, because the rail was round and so thin—but all of a sudden this warmth overcame me and this gust of wind got me on the ground again. Yeah, there are too many things that have happened in my life to just call them coincidences. Someone did not want me to die. I should have died many times.

I'VE BEEN sober almost two years, and I like myself now. I have a lot more respect for myself than I did. My sobriety is the most important thing in my life. It comes before everything. Anything I have now wouldn't be worth a damn if I wasn't sober. I'd lose everything. No fun. I don't want to go back. I'll graduate from high school this year. I love school. I want to go into the psychology field. I'll be good at it too. I mean, I've been through almost everything. I've been told that a good thing comes out of every bad thing that happens—like knowledge. I think I could help people going through the stuff that happened to me, turn it around into a good thing to help others.

Ralph

LET ME BOIL IT DOWN FOR YOU: peace with yourself. To me that's it. Not necessarily with the outside world, but with yourself. All I have in the world is myself. That's all I have when I arrive in the world, and when I leave again. I don't mean that in a self-centered way, it's just a biological fact. For me recovery allows me to be at peace with myself. That's the most tangible reward. Also I find that my emotions and feelings get more clear and real. That doesn't necessarily mean good or happy, but more real. I've been able to cry recently. I don't see it when I'm in the middle of it, but sometimes the most difficult things are the best things. Like I didn't cry about losing a mother at age six, but it's better to cry about it now than never.

SOMEBODY TOLD me once that the word *spirituality* means "Existence on an elevated plateau." Well, I'm existing on an elevated plateau now, and getting there meant keeping my mind open. Honest to God, I never thought that I would pray. Spirituality is a very personal thing. It's between you and God, Buddha, Allah, doorknob, whatever. I feel fortunate to have been led very early in my recovery to Native American spirituality. That's a spirituality that's very palatable to me. The people who stay sober and get changed are the ones who find themselves. But anything that is forcing me into a dogmatic kind of conformity ain't going to work. It never did, and it never will. I've gotten more rebellious than before I got clean. Still, today I try to respect other people's beliefs to the point where they don't impinge on me, and that's great.

I WRITE and play music and have a little record label with some people, and so everything's going great. If I find that my understanding of spirituality doesn't necessarily coexist with being in a band and playing for people that are fucked up every night, I don't have to deal with the industry. It's a real breeding ground for that kind of shit. But right now, I'm not in a big hurry to make decisions. Success to me is relative. My own understanding of success has to do with my love of life, of other human beings, and of myself. I don't mean that in a narcissistic, self-centered way. Everything else is just stuff. So for anybody reading this thing: If you're having a hard time, so am I. So is everybody. Somebody told me to not pray for an easy life but to pray for the strength and courage to find the thing, whatever it is, that fits you. I know people who got clean just by sitting up in the mountains and meditating or whatever. It might not have worked for me, but the point is to be open and not give up.

Jennifer

SOBRIETY, I LOVE IT. It's my life. It's brought me back together with my daughter. It's brought us closer. I abandoned her when she was four years old. My mother had died recently and I didn't know how to express my feelings, so I went into drugs. I abandoned my daughter to use because I was just so out of it. All I wanted to do was do drugs so I could forget. Toward the end of my addiction it made me paranoid, it made me scared, it made me ugly.

I GOT arrested for selling to an undercover agent, and while I was there for thirty days, on Rikers Island, I called up an old friend of mine and I asked him, "What should I do? I don't know what to do. I don't want to stay here—I don't want to get sent upstate someplace." So he said, Why don't you call a therapeutic community. You know, so that's what I did. I spoke to a social worker in jail, and I told him that I didn't want to stay here, that my problem was drug abuse. Not selling drugs, but drug abuse. So he said okay; he set it up for someone to come and represent me in the courtroom when I had to go. And they came from the therapeutic community and were present in the courtroom at my court date and spoke to the judge. The judge asked me what did I want to do, and I said I wanted to go into a therapeutic community 'cause that's what I need. I'm

a drug addict and I need help. So he said okay, and he gave me five years' probation. I was very lucky that I didn't get killed. And there were lots of instances where I could have been murdered. I used to think, "Dear God, don't let me get killed. Don't let me die."

BEING SOBER has given me my daughter, and that's the most important thing. But it's also given me structure. Being drug-free, I have structure and I have a direction in my life. It has changed my life because now I'm very selective instead of just accepting what comes my way. I'm very choosy. The change is within me, you know. I don't choose to be around negative people. I don't choose to go to negative places.

I THINK people who get into sobriety should stay in sobriety. I believe that all it takes is one day at a time. That's all it takes. It's true. It's one day at a time, but you have to do it, not picking up. I was married, and my husband died while I was in sobriety, and I didn't pick up. I just kept talking about it, talking about how much I missed him and how sorry I was that he died. I just didn't pick up. If you stay in recovery, you'll see that your life changes and it gets better, you know, it really does.

Joel

LIFE HAS BEEN VERY FRUSTRATING the last few years. I've had a lot of health issues. I look at life since 1991, and I really feel that until things stabilize for a while, I'm doing damage control more than recovery. I don't have the cheerful recovery story that so many people have. The "I got into recovery, I got a good job, and I'm going to live happily ever after." I'm very blunt about it. It's been very painful and difficult. But the point that I make when I talk about it, is that I didn't go out and get loaded over this shit.

THE MOST immediate thing is that if I haven't found a job within the next month, I'll be living on air. For some people there are long-term things, but I don't have long-term because of my health issues. I'm trying to deal with the short term. I'm an attorney. I was in legal publishing for many years. I had a temporary job earlier this year with an ADA advocate firm—an Americans with Disabilities Advocacy firm—which is the most fun I've ever had with a law degree. So I'd like to stay in that field, but the job market is tough; everybody wants lawyers, nobody has money. My concept of addiction is not so much about the substance you use. It's about the whole personality. I was an addict long before I got high. I was compulsive; I was running from the things that hurt and doing anything that would turn off my feelings. As a child, I was a bookworm and into junk food. In adult life it means being a workaholic. Gambling, junkies, guys who blow their rent money in Vegas, what have you. I suppose diving into hobbies obsessively—if I spent twenty hours a day on the Internet, that would be addictive behavior. But I was running from pain a long time before I discovered getting high. And even though it's been six years since I got high, all of those behavior patterns are still waiting in the wings.

A BIG part of my sobriety is fighting the fear. Especially the last few years. Nineteen ninety was a good year, and then I got my hopes up. Going through three major medical situations, that just took four years out of my life. I'm afraid to get happy. It's like if I get happy like I did in 1990, I'll get smacked again. So it's still the childhood thought pattern: If I stick up too high, I'll get knocked down. So dealing with the fear is a constant. It's like I'm wrestling with my gremlins all the time.

Susan

I WORK AT THE TENDERLOIN AIDS Resource Center. I'm a community-health outreach worker. I go out on the street and talk to people about HIV, safe sex, risk reduction, and I distribute condoms and bleach. Most people on the street are pretty good about using bleach, yet they keep using drugs. They're not interested in stopping or in making major changes in their lives. I've learned in this work and in my own life that if a person doesn't want it, there's nothing you can do to help them. Sometimes people are forced to change, but it doesn't last. It has to come from within.

SOMETIMES THEY say, "Hey, condom lady" when I walk by. Gradually, though, I get to know some of them and they remember my name. I like what I do. It's very rewarding. At first I didn't know if it would be dangerous, but it isn't. People are friendlier than I thought. They appreciate it when someone treats them like a human being. Since we've been doing this outreach program in this city—having needle exchanges, giving out condoms and bleach—it has really reduced the incidence of HIV in the drug-using population. In some cities where they don't have outreach programs like this, the HIV incidence among drug users is 60 percent and higher. Here it's about 15 percent.

WHEN I see all these people, I know that I'm not any better than them. I know that I could be right back where they are if I started using again. It makes me very grateful for what I have since I got clean. I remember what it was like to have my world just get smaller and smaller. I remember hating myself more and more. I remember getting sick of feeling like I had nothing else to look forward to except the next hit. I remember wanting to kill myself. Using was slow suicide.

NOW I'M doing something that means a great deal to me. I feel like it's what I'm meant to do. A year and a half of being clean and it's not so hard to stay clean. It's a habit now, a way of life. It's not something I take for granted. But I've learned how addiction affected every facet of my life, and I've started to heal some of those things.

I DIDN'T know what life would be like when I got clean. I was afraid it would be boring. But I knew I had to try it. It was that or die. I've been happier than I've ever been. I have hope, feel freer than I've ever felt. I have real friendships, and I laugh more than I ever laughed when I got high. I don't know what's going to happen in the future, but I know I'll be okay. I know that I can feel good about myself and be excited about what life will bring.

Michael

I WAS ALWAYS LOOKING FORWARD to the next new thing, to be part of everything. I hung out with gay people, straight people, artists, punkers, mods, and I was very popular because I could buy the alcohol and I knew who had the drugs. But I'd be lying to you if I said it felt really wonderful and that everything was fun. There's that great line, that "everything was fun, then it was fun with problems, then it was problems." I'd say, I'm not an addict, because I don't drink as much as they do, or I don't do as many drugs as they do, or I do different kinds. . . . Deep in denial. The severity was ominous.

I DIDN'T feel for the first, maybe, three years of my recovery. I didn't allow myself to express a feeling at all. When I came in, there were just two identifiable feelings—craziness and panic—and I was angry as all hell. And I couldn't figure out why. I had this problem with breaking down and telling people, "I'm in pain." I was always this upstanding man, and I thought I could handle anything. To be honest, I couldn't handle it, but I gave a great show. When I finally said, "I give up. Somebody show me what to do," they told me, "Well, the first thing you can do is just get angry." And I went to a psychologist and that helped me immensely, to accept that it's okay to be angry, it's okay to be upset, it's okay having joy in my life.

SOME OF the barriers that I faced in recovery are the same that I faced when I was using, but I didn't let myself deal with them. It's obvious that I'm black, but I'm also gay. So when I was using it was like a novelty, and I was your token black gay friend. And when I got sober, I was the token black gay person in recovery. If I was just black or just gay that would be one thing, but you can't be both in this society. So you're clean and sober, go hang out with other gay people in recovery. But I didn't get any support there. The irony is that I got the most support from bikers in recovery—people who felt alienated because they were who they were. We have a kinship that is unimaginable. One barrier I had to overcome was, while I didn't give a shit if people thought that I was different, I had to get over it for me. That was the most difficult part. Just the idea that I'm different by birthright bugged me.

IT TOOK me a long time to realize that I am 100 percent human and everything in my life is meant to be—including my mistakes. For years I thought that I had to be something else. It finally dawned on me a few years ago when this old redneck, who was about sixty years old, was yelling at the top of his lungs that his name was such-and-such and that he was an alcoholic and a human being. That touched a nerve in me, and I realized that I am first and foremost, regardless of where I came from, a human being. It doesn't matter what anyone else thinks of me. It doesn't matter what clothes I wear or what I own, I'm not better or worse than anybody else. That is the greatest gift of my life, and my sobriety. To be positive, to be negative, but whatever it is, feel what I need to feel, do as I need to do, but above all to be human. It feels so good. I like that idea, it makes me smile.

Iris and Jimmy

Iris I remember there was one time that stands out. Jimmy and I had only one car, with no registration, no insurance, no money, but it was the only transportation that we had at the time. So I had to go cop, and then I was supposed to bring some dope back for both of us—but it didn't work out the way it was supposed to. So I said, "Well, I'll shoot this now, and I'll be straight, and I'll be able to get more money." But it didn't happen that way at all. And so again, I was able to get more money, but only enough for me, and so I said, "Well, I'll do this, and then I'll get some more money." Anyhow, by the time I got back to where Jimmy was waiting for me at home, it had been two or three days. He was in deep withdrawal. And even though I knew that, it was more important for me to be straight than it was for me to get back there and help him out. I knew that he was going to be in withdrawal and that he couldn't leave because I had taken the only car. He had no choice. He had to stay there.

Jimmy There were lots of times when we looked at each other and said, "This is it, we gotta do something." It happened all the time. After a while, the misery got to be so obvious and pronounced that you couldn't deny that it was going on, but I got desensitized. I was always aware that it was a bad deal, but I was in such denial that I accepted it. There were times when I just knew that it was all wrong. There were lots of horrible experiences. I remember looking through the window of a jail and seeing Iris being locked up. I had a sense of loss, but the truth is, I realized that I didn't want to have to go out and get drugs on my own again. I'm getting honest about that. There was lots of despair and shit in that kind of addiction.

Iris I didn't go into treatment because I wanted to deal with being HIV-positive or because I wanted to stay alive. It wasn't about that. I went into treatment and tried to get clean because I was sick and tired of living like that. I just didn't believe that I could get up one more day and do this over and over for the rest of my life. After I got sober, I didn't start dealing with HIV until I really had a good grip on my addiction—because, really, HIV wasn't going to take me out. I knew that it wasn't. It was addiction that was going to do me in. So I went to treatment, and I've been clean since that day. But I worked on my addiction first. I didn't really start working on HIV and dealing with it until nine months later. I started looking at it and the possibility that I might die from this disease, and these other issues that I have to deal with: My father got cancer and died since I got clean. That made me take a good look at my own mortality. I realized that if I didn't use, I'd be okay. Still, AIDS really brings it home. You have to live one day at a time or you are going to go crazy.

Jimmy You want the honest reason why I got sober? Intervention. I was living in the woods. I had secondary stages of syphilis. I had pneumonia. I was HIV-positive. I was homeless.

I was wearing two coats. I had turned into the very thing I had seen as a kid. I had turned into a bum. You see, when I was eight years old, I remember seeing this guy covered with leaves being put in a police car, and the policeman's face as they stuck him in the car. I remember asking my mom, "Why are they treating this person like that?" I was real confused as a kid. And she said, "That's because he's a bum." I had never heard the term before. So I said, "What is a bum?" And she said, "Well, it's a person who doesn't have a home, who doesn't work, and who drinks all day long." And that's the person that

I turned into. I think I wanted, finally, to live and not be doing the things I was doing anymore. In any case, it was an intervention. My mom came to Florida and paid an addict to find me in the woods. It was pathetic. I went into a treatment center up in Manhattan and then came down here and started my journey.

Iris Today, my spirituality means a lot to me and it has nothing to do with religion. As far as religion, I had negative experiences. So when I came into recovery, I really had to develop my own beliefs. Spirituality to me is feeling connected to everybody and everything else. I really believe that I'm not a human being having a spiritual experience. I'm a spiritual being having a human experience. And once we have that experience, we go on. Spirituality is that feeling of just being connected to everyone else. That happens whenever I'm counseling somebody in treatment. When I feel connected, I understand why, because we always ask, "Why did I have to go through this?" But now I realize that all that was meant to happen; it was for a purpose. And I get in touch with that all the time. Every time I can share my own experience and help someone, then I know why.

Jimmy I'll give you an example of a spiritual experience. It was in New Jersey; it was the fall, and the leaves were falling off the trees. We were living in this cardboard thing, and I got up one morning. Iris was still sleeping. She got up behind me and heard me say, "Isn't this beautiful?" I was admiring what a beautiful day it was, and she was struck by how nuts I must have been to look around and see this as a beautiful setting. We had a dinette under a mulberry tree, a door that was cut out of cardboard that other addicts were sick enough to come over and knock on, to have permission to come in. It was just crazy. And so here I was thinking, "This is dynamite, being in tune with nature and shit." That's denial and that's okay, because spirituality is being able to be in tune with the good around you. I've gotten spiritual messages from the weirdest places. I got them from people who were younger than me, from people who had less than me, from people who I always saw myself as being better than. But it wasn't until I got sober that I was able to open this part of me that was able to accept good things from everybody that offered them. It's nuts.

Darlyn

FREEDOM TODAY IS MUCH MORE like an open field, and before it was more like a small box. The fact is there are so many things in life, and as I continue to get sober, there are more and more options open to me as to how my day can go. Even when the day is not going good and I feel that things are a little bit against me, there is always a resounding peace underneath it all. When I was getting high, I believed that things would always be against me. I would always be pushing up against society, against my idea of success, against what I felt I needed to be in order to be a whole person, and I don't feel that way at all now. Today I can sit and have a pleasant time and be present. I can sit with someone like you and not feel like I have to be somewhere else. Very small things like that keep me sober every day.

SOBRIETY, REALLY, is standing still and sticking my hand out and saying, Hello my name is Darlyn—and that the reaction doesn't define who I am. Whereas before, I only lived in other people's eyes. It was only reaction that defined me. If I was making you laugh, then I was funny; if you were checking me out, then I was beautiful. I can get up in the morning and do the simplest things, whether take my time or rush to get

somewhere, but I still feel whole and I don't feel as though I'm leaving parts of myself in other places. Everything's walking together now.

WHEN I got sober, I went to see a friend get a year cake, and I was so astounded that anybody could get a year off drugs and alcohol. I remember the first time that she had thirty days clean, and I was floored by that. Thirty days, Jesus, that was an extremely long time for me. And I still believe that. I think that anybody that chooses to make that choice, that one day, two days, three days—that's a long period of time. Forty-eight hours off of something that has been holding you up, propping you up like a big dummy. It is literally like coming through the weeds and out of the fog. You know it's just this tiny, tiny pinhole of faith that has grown into this whole world that is now available to me. The willingness to strip yourself down, to change your behavior and admit your behavior, are amazing things; and even though they sound foreign, in the long run I can see how amazing it was. They really were blind steps toward sanity and peace of mind. That was what I strived for most: Peace of mind. Just to be quiet in my head. That's it.

Meg

WHEN I WAS SMOKING POT, I thought it was a choice. I thought I was crazy and depressed, and I thought society was against me. I had a really weird way of looking at things. I really thought I was insane. When I got sober, my mind started to clear, and I found that I wasn't as insane as I thought I was. I realized that it was the drugs that made me feel insane. Drugs hindered me in so many ways, and I ran around proud of the fact that I was doing them. I didn't think I was a drug addict. I thought drugs were great and human beings should do them, but when I stopped for a while I realized, "My God, they're like 98 percent of the problem!" I had spoken to a few people about it, and addiction goes way beyond using. Addiction is just a side effect of the disease. Why do we use? Why do we pick up? I know that for me it was because I felt insecure, and I felt down. My niche, my security, whatever you want to call it, was drugs. They kept everything in check. But essentially it made everything worse and it snowballed.

AFTER SIX months of staying sober, when I decided on this rebellious action—two long puffs off a joint—it made me feel really shitty again. Even though it wasn't this long-drawn-out period, it was like, "Wow, I haven't felt this kind of depression in months." It was really hard-core. I even found myself back into thinking that everyone's against me. The paranoia was a hell of a lot stronger. Although pot wasn't my drug of choice, it was cocaine, it was inevitable that if I continued to smoke pot, I would pick up a bottle of Jack Daniel's, and I would do a few lines, and before you know it, I'd be back into the whole scene. I really accepted what people had to say, and I really accepted that I just can't use drugs and alcohol. It's just not for me.

BEING SOBER isn't always easy, but things get better. Now there are things in my life that I love. I love my job. I got into a baccalaureate program at Macalester, I'm going to get licensed to teach, and I want to get involved in art therapy and use art as a means of recovery, not just for drugs and addiction but with terminally ill cases. I can do so many things now. I know so much. I mean, your life doesn't just snowball into shit. Normal people who aren't addicts have problems and deal with them. Addicts have a tendency to deal with problems differently, and that's the biggest part of getting sober. We have to learn how to change. We have to change how we deal with things. Because I can guarantee you, before anyone picked up, they dealt with things very irrationally or they got very sad or frustrated or they masked how they felt. Now it's like, I can feel shitty and that's okay. There's no reason for it; it's not a government conspiracy. No one's out to get Meg, you know? It's just, I'm having a bad day. And as long as I make it to work and meet my responsibilities and not crawl into a ball and sleep it off, I'll be okay.

Mark

WHEN I FIRST GOT SOBER, one of my basic issues was how to deal with anxiety and stress without taking a chemical. I think that, speaking for myself, not only did I have a fear of my own anxiety, but I think I feared strong emotions of any kind. It was like I had a phobia to any strong feelings. In treatment there are a lot of things that bring up strong emotions. You're scared that they will destroy you, but you learn how to get through them and not be annihilated by them. You learn that you bounce back and you can handle a lot more than you think you can handle. I think that that was the most important thing that I got out of treatment—that I'm capable of a lot more than I think I'm capable of, in terms of handling my emotions and in terms of forming intimate relationships with other people.

THE BEST thing about being sober is just knowing that you are doing the right thing, because you know that you are living the right way. Back when I was using drugs and alcohol for every kind of problem, I knew that this was not going to last forever and that ultimately there's going to be horrible consequences, even if it might be effective in the short run. There was always the fear in the back of my mind of running out of the drugs, and just a lot of fear in general that I'm free of now.

Now I'm able to fully realize my potential as a human being and do the things in life that I've wanted to do, and maybe even have some aptitude and skill in doing them. I work as a psychologist. I actually have three jobs right now! Two of them are research and one is psychological assessment. There is some fear and anxiety because some of the jobs rely on grants, which are limited by time, but I never would have been able to pursue them if I was using. I'm just trying to be the most complete and integrated person that I can be—which is impossible when you are loaded all the time.

CAN ANYBODY get sober? I think it's dependent on the degree to which they want help. Do they feel that they have suffered enough? That's a very subjective question, because for one person, acting inappropriately at a cocktail party could be the bottom, and another person could lose everything and still that's not enough to compel them to enter sobriety or attempt sobriety. My own experience was an extended period of time spent in a protective environment of treatment, so I am very biased. What I know is that people that stay sober tend to form relationships with other recovering people and follow the examples of those that have gone before them—at least that was my experience.

Mary

I DON'T KNOW. It's like, "Is the American dream working?" It's a nice idea, but I don't believe it. I want to believe that everyone can get clean, but I've seen a lot of people try and then they die. Still, I think that if you keep yourself surrounded by people who know you and know who you are and you're honest, your odds are really good.

ADDICTION IS more than a disease. When I read the characteristics of an alcoholic or addict, I had those before I ever started using. I felt like an outsider, I felt different from other people, and it seemed like I felt things more strongly than other people. Even as a kid, I would try to be whatever people wanted me to be. I was totally intrigued by the whole rock and roll and sex and drugs that went along with that. That was the stuff that I liked. It wasn't like I said, "I'm going to go out and be a drug addict." I said, "I'm going to go out and be wild and meet all these interesting people." But that didn't happen, and like a lot of addicts, I wasn't kicking back with all my friends. I was in a little tiny room with drugs and myself. I would always just use until I passed out. I used to OD all the time, and someone would revive me. I thought, I might die one of these times in this little room and no one is going to save me. And that's not too glamorous; that's just kind of pathetic.

EVENTUALLY IT got to the point where I couldn't drown out the voices anymore. I mean, I knew that the gig was up and that I could only do this for so long and then either get clean or disappear. There was no way that I could pull it off financially, and I had a lot of guilt. I'd been through treatment before, and everyone had bent over backwards for me. I wasn't sure if there would be another chance after this. I had been told by a lot of people that there wouldn't be another chance. After a few weeks of sobriety, I started feeling a sense of hope. There were a few people that actually made me feel like I could do it. Everyone else was too scared to have faith anymore. I remember my dad saying, "She's just one of those people that isn't going to get it." It made me feel angry, kind of rebellious, like "I'll show you!" I also felt sad and ashamed. I think it took a while for me to start feeling good. I felt like a zombie more than anything else for a long time. I didn't laugh or cry, I just kind of trudged.

LIFE TODAY is pretty simple. I have a job that I like. I work with flowers—I'm a floral designer. I get to work with my hands and that is great. I make things. It's really healing for me. It calms my neurotic brain. So I do that, I hang out with my friends, I do normal stuff. There are still things that I feel are taking too long to happen, but for the most part, I'm okay.

Lee

SO I WENT TO TREATMENT at the VA hospital. That's when I started to deal with these issues from the war and find out that it was okay to be a Vietnam veteran and be comfortable with yourself. I don't have to carry no shame or nothing or hide all these feelings. When I got back people spit on us. It was like all this weight, thousands of pounds, was lifted off of me. I could sit in this room with all these Vietnam veterans and feel what they were talking about. All these hurts and pains these guys were carrying. Someone could understand me, and I could understand them. I don't know if it was a spiritual awakening, but it was a change in my life. I don't have to hold all this hurt and distrust and resentment. I still get that today, a lot of helpless feelings. It's probably from the war when I held guys in my arms and they'd say, "Help me, it hurts!" or they'd call out for their mother, "Mom!" And then the next minute they're laying there dead. You get angry; you get that helpless feeling. It affects me today when things happen.

I GOT married in 1983 and stayed in that relationship for almost six years. It was an unhealthy relationship on both sides. The whole marriage I was drinking—couldn't sober up. There was a lot of power and control in that relationship. When I got out of that relationship, I got sober and I got okay with myself. After we got divorced, I took the kids, a boy and a girl, in 1990, and I've been raising them ever since.

GETTING SOBER was a lot of work. I needed to be honest with myself and with others. That was the key to my sobriety. And dealing with some issues from the war. I still have a lot to deal with there. It's been a long, tough road, but since I got sober in 1989 up to today, my life has gone in a complete circle. When I got divorced, my wife took everything from me—my children, my home, my car. I didn't have nothing. I got employed in August of 1989, and I've worked ever since. I'm working as an advocate in a halfway house. I work with job placement, schooling, help for the court systems. I bought my own home, I have my own car, I have my children, I have a fiancée and there's mutual respect there—but my sobriety is still the main thing.

ONE THING I would like to share is that there are a lot of Indian alcoholics, being Vietnam veterans. And they're denying themselves the chance to deal with these things. I've offered that help. It's out there. And they say, "I don't want to deal with it. I don't want to talk about it." They do the same thing I did. When I sobered up, I wanted to help people. That is what my sobriety is all about. My boy asked me, "I need a hand." I said, "Remember you got two of them. One's for helping yourself, the other's for helping others." He just looked at me and started laughing so hard. I said, that's what I do—help myself and others.

Sandra

I NEVER THOUGHT there was a better way of life. I grew up thinking that's what life was—that when you got older you drank. That's what my parents did. Everybody around me did it. I thought that was what I was supposed to do. It was fun, at first. I started drinking when I was about ten. By the time I was twelve, I ran away. I felt safer out on the streets, and people liked me more on the streets.

ON THE streets we took care of each other—took care of each other's drug use, that is. When I look back, I see a lonely, scared kid. But if I didn't have alcohol and drugs at that time, I probably would have killed myself. The drugs and alcohol made me forget, made me somebody I thought I wanted to be. When I see kids now who are ten, eleven, and twelve, like I was, it makes me sick that nobody was there to protect me.

WHAT MADE me decide to get sober was that the alcohol and drugs weren't helping anymore. Memories of my child-hood kept coming back—thoughts of being sexually abused and hit a lot—and nothing took them away no matter how drunk I got. So I called up the county—because I didn't have any money—and they sent me to treatment. I was at a cross-roads, you know, where I had only three choices: kill myself, keep drinking and die slowly, or change. I'm real stubborn, and people told me I'd never make it, so I got sober.

I DO hair now, and one of my clients was telling me about her daughter who is deaf. She got a hearing aid to help her hear, but she wouldn't wear it because the noise was too terrifying for her. That's kind of how I felt when I first got sober. Being sober brought back all the feelings I never felt before. It terri-fied me.

I ALSO got sober because of my son. He's been through a lot. He was thirteen or fourteen when I went into treat-ment. His life was unmanageable, and he didn't know how to trust people. He's going to be nineteen this month. But I noticed after I started cleaning up, he started changing too. I'm sure he has a lot of resentment toward me. I mean, it used to be like he was the parent and I was the child. I'd tell him I'd be home in an hour and come home two days later sometimes. I hurt an innocent life. I became like my father, and I didn't like that. But our relationship has gotten better. He respects me now. He didn't respect me before.

CONFIDENCE. YOU get a lot of confidence being sober. It's shown me that I can do anything. I'm not living in fear any-more. Who knows, I might be president someday, own IBM, but it goes beyond just that. I'm happy. I'm a miracle, you know.

Candacy

WELL, WHEN I FIRST GOT CLEAN I said all I wanted was my own apartment, my cat, and to go to school and hang out. And I got it all so quickly, I was amazed. I thought it would take years to get to a standing point and feel normal, whatever that means. Things are better every day. I've had some downfalls in recovery and had some really shitty things happen to me, but in general the progression of my life is just amazing. I work in a business center at a hotel. It's beautiful and amazing that I work there. I work with a lot of CEOs who are really stressed. Working under that kind of pressure, I have to learn patience to provide the service that they need. Through my job, I realize that other people's stress level is theirs, and I don't have to buy into it.

SOMETIMES WHEN something happens, I'm like, "Oh, God, am I going to use over this?" I've had some good excuses to use. They say in your first year of sobriety not to get into a relationship, but I did. He'd been in recovery for about six months, and for some reason the relationship wasn't very healthy. There was a lot of emotional dependency on each other. I broke up with him because I knew that I was going to school full-time, and he was way too dependent on me. So we talked about it and broke up, and the next day he decided to blow his brains out. I had a lot of guilt around that. I had no idea how to deal with it. I didn't want to use, but at the same time, I didn't want to feel. I'm grateful that I had people in my life to help me through, because, as I said, it would have been a great excuse. But I really feel that if I use again, I will die.

I KNOW from my own story that there's a really fine line in life. I was totally into needles. That was my habit. It was supposed to be the best day. I actually had a smaller dosage than I usually do, but I started to feel shitty and realized, "Oh, shit, something's really wrong." I passed out. I was lying there, my eyes were open, and I was psychotic—I was hearing voices. I touched my hand and it was freezing cold, and my head started to spin—and I'm wondering what's going to happen next. Am I overdosing? Is anybody going to find me? I really didn't want to die. I wasn't one of those addicts who wanted to shoot up until they die. I felt like I was enhancing my life by using drugs. I saw bright visions of reds, blues, and purples, and they wrapped themselves around me. I was going through this tunnel. Everything was moving really fast. I still don't understand what happened. I heard my sister and my mother back in Columbus. My sister was a biology major, and she was telling me things that I didn't know, like to lie on my stomach because it put the least amount of pressure on my heart, and to try to keep breathing. My mother was crying, "Oh my God, we're losing her." So I'm like, "Oh, fuck, I don't want to die." I was twenty-two years old and felt really cheated, way too young to die. It was this vision, this realization that what I'm doing is going to kill me—that all the years of using were coming to this. That was my spiritual awakening. I just surrendered and said, "You know what, God? I can't do this anymore. I'll do anything, anything to stop."

Lowell

WHY ISN'T THERE A CURE? I think you'd be talking about curing human nature, and it's not that simplistic. No one thing is going to cure it. Why do they call it a disease? Because it's got a lot of the same symptoms: it's chronic, it gets worse and not better, and it has a set of predictable symptoms that lead to either insanity or death.

IT TOOK me nine years to stay sober six months. I had tried religion. I believed in a cult at one time. I tried the Christian religious experiences, the fundamentalist religious experience—and so I had been trying for a long time. Getting sober wasn't one specific experience but rather a series of incidents. I remember, and this is so simplistic, but it really touched me, I was watching a television show on alcohol and drug abuse, and this guy said, "Let me put it this way. If not drinking or using would improve the quality of your life, then drinking or using is a problem." It sounds so stupid, but it just triggered it. I had been praying for years every night to get help. Every night I did it.

NOW I'M a counseling supervisor at a treatment center. I've done countless kinds of after-care groups and done work in prisons and all over, and I still have no fucking idea why people get sober. End of story. I mean, in the end, there are some unanswerable parts for all of us. I'll tell you a great story. I was in institutions a lot as a kid. You can imagine. And I had this friend, David. We used to get locked up together over and over and over. We were in a reformatory, and I was always getting into trouble. There are all these internal problems in institutions, and I'd get mixed up in that. David, on the other hand, was a great inmate. He did really well in jail. And they'd always pull me aside and give me the "You're going to be a convict for life" speech. And they'd say, "Well, David's doing really well, we're going to let him go home." They'd try to shame me with that stuff. The last I had heard of him, he was pouring boiling water on his arms to get narcotics from the prison hospital. I'd say, out of the past thirty years, he's probably done twenty-five in prison. Why him and not me? I was probably much more evil than him. Why did I get out and not him? Well, you might say, "Well, you were more honest and responsible and you were willing to pay the price." But why? I don't know. I think there are some questions that can't be answered.

Lee

I'M A CERTIFIED COUNSELOR for chemical dependency. I work mostly with Hispanic people. I've seen a lot of patients relapse or die, or both. The other day, in fact, we had one. We've had him around for two or three years, and we've tried everything with him, different treatment programs. The other night they found him dead. That was sad, to see him deteriorate so rapidly. But usually the people who come in here are people who have to. They've got pressure on them. They're usually referrals from the legal system. They got arrested, usually for DWI or domestic violence or something that got them in trouble with the law. And those are very difficult. Because, first of all, they don't think that they have any problems except with the police. There's a lot of denial; none of them are convinced. They think their problems are legal and don't got to do with the drugs or alcohol that they're taking.

I KNOW about denial. One of my consequences was that I ended up in prison. I had gotten a fifteen-to-twenty-year sentence. I was there for seven years, three months, and twenty-three days. Going to jail didn't get me sober. We'd get loaded all the time. Mostly marijuana. We'd call it cotton. I never thought that I had a problem. It was part of living, getting loaded. That was what we looked forward to. I didn't know it was an illness, much less a disease. I thought that was just a lifestyle. My family was all into alcohol. My father was having a lot of problems, my mother, my sister, all the neighbors and everybody used to drink, and I thought that was just the thing to do.

AFTER I got sober, I was leading a whole new life. I wanted to give some of that away to my friends who were still active. Some of them saw that change in me, and that impressed them a lot. And they wanted to do likewise. For instance, a lot of guys that I knew in prison or when I was on the streets as a full-blown alkie, they'd wake up and they'd see me in the detox, and a lot of them would think I was one of them. That I was in there for detoxification purposes, and that I had on my civilian clothes because I was on the way out. And when they found out that I was sober and that I was a counselor there, they really freaked out about it. Some of them were amazed, and some of them wanted to do the same thing. And a lot of them did.

Kim

JESSA GIVES ME SOMETHING TO FOCUS ON, something to work for. She gives me something to think about so I don't just sit here and whimper about my own problems in my little pity hole. It's not just me anymore. If I mess up or am too drunk to see what's going on, look at what I could lose. I look at her and I see so much hope, so much that I didn't have. I want her to have a safe, sober environment so she can come to me and feel safe. I can't fathom abandoning her, forcing her to grow up that way. I can't understand how a mom can do that to her children. I know there's a reason, but it bothers me. Getting drunk isn't even an option anymore. It's just not.

I'M GRATEFUL that I didn't have to lose everything in my life before I got sober. I mean, I lost some friends, trust, respect, but nothing on the level that other people have. Because my mom grew up with alcoholics, she knew the signs early on. She saw what I was becoming, and she wanted to do what she could to stop it before I started going through all these awful consequences. She wanted to get me help right away, and she got me help.

I WASN'T ready, though. I was sober for fourteen months, then I started hanging out with my drinking friends again and started drinking. I finally got sober again March 7 of 1993. I became pregnant with Jessa in August of 1993. It was hard to stay sober when I found out I was pregnant. It was my first big crisis, but I knew it wasn't going to go away if I started drinking. I stayed sober with the help of her father, my family, and the school. Up until the time I had her, I still acted really immature and irresponsible, but when I had her I said, "I'm a mom now and I have to get my act together." And I did. I try real hard to be a mom and do the mom things. She wasn't planned, but given the opportunity—knowing what I know now—I wouldn't change a thing. I never want to give her up.

I DON'T miss being a kid because I never really was a kid. When I was a kid, I was always around adults, so I don't know what being a kid is like. I like being a mom and an adult and doing all the adult things. In fact, I'm kind of a tomboy. I like to do guy things—play around with cars, motorcycles, digging around the garage and things.

I'D RATHER hang out in a garage with a bunch of guys, getting my hands dirty on a car, than go to the mall with a bunch of girls to buy things. It'd be cool to be a girl mechanic. I'm pretty good at it, too. I can replace a valve-cover gasket, replace brakes, change oil, and overhaul a carburetor. Now that I've graduated from high school, I'm seriously considering going to tech school to take a mechanics course. You never know. Stranger things happen.

Jude

MY DAD DIED SEVERAL YEARS AGO. He was a drug addict and an alcoholic, but he never quit. I got to make my peace with him like three days before he passed away. What a trip. When I was a kid, we fought a lot. He didn't live at home, but he was in the neighborhood all the time. When I was fifteen, we were getting loaded together, and I came out of a blackout with a knife in my hand. I had stabbed him thirteen times. After the stabbing we never communicated, even after I got sober. When he started dying, everyone told me I ought to go see him, but I didn't want to. I hated him. But my family kept bugging me, and finally, a couple of sober friends said I should do it. So I went, and he was in intensive care and incoherent. My mom said I should hold his hand, and if he recognizes me, he'll squeeze my hand once for yes and twice for no. When I did that, she said his eyes showed recognition. It was weird, because I've never touched that man in anything but a violent way my whole life, and when I touched him, it was like a skeleton's hand. As I held his hand, I started getting emotional. I didn't know what to say to him. He was squeezing my hand, and I didn't know if he was trying to tell me something. I asked him if he loved me, and he squeezed my hand, yeah. It hit me right then that I didn't hate him, that I was just like him. We were both drug addicts and alcoholics. We could only do what was in our natures. The hate went away, and I told him I loved him. I hung around a little bit, and then I left. That was it. He died three days later. Felt good to make the peace with him.

WHEN I was using, it was insane. I went blind when I was eighteen. I had just gotten out of jail, started doing some catch-up partying. I was in a bar when a fight broke out, and somebody hit me in the face with a pool stick. A week later I was in the hospital getting my retina patched. I was already blind in my left eye from when I had spinal meningitis as a kid. Now I find that the peace is in my head. I was consumed with hate and anger and terror. Terror is what brought me to my knees. It was with me every waking moment. And now I don't have it. It's like, when I go out now, I'm not tense. I just go out and do whatever I want to do. I have some social skills now, which I never had before. Probably because I didn't like anybody. I was scared, but I just didn't know how to communicate with normal people.

George

THE GUY that raised me was an alcoholic. From the third grade of school on, we lived together, just he and I, and we'd spend our nights in the bars. Being with an alcoholic, everybody was a drinker and everybody got in trouble. I just figured that was the place in life that I was supposed to be.

LATER, I started working in Cleveland. We had a place where we'd cash our checks down on skid row. We'd be spending money down there with the stew bums at the end of the bar. I'd say to the bartender, "Buy them a bottle of wine and let them enjoy themselves. Poor bastards, if they had a trade like me, they wouldn't be bums." My attitude was that they were bums, and I was a great adventurer. Inside, I knew that I had a problem, but it was a part of myself that I lost sight of, because of my alcoholic thinking.

ONE OF the first miracles of my recovery happened when I was with some sober people, and I balanced a quarter on the table. The steadiness that I had to do that caused me to cry. Because two months before, when I went into detox, I thought I was going to kill myself. I figured, I'm dying anyway, I'll let the doctor do what he wants. There was no thought in my mind of recovery. The family doctor had been telling me

for years to go into recovery. I was in detox for fourteen days. Thank God I couldn't walk. If I could have, I would have just walked out. But I couldn't. I couldn't hold my food; I was just a shaken mess.

TWO YEARS earlier I had dried out for a month when I had open-heart surgery, but at the end of the month I started drinking again. I asked the heart specialist if a little drink would hurt me—"No it won't bother you." Three weeks later I was back at work and drinking heavily again. I couldn't stop. Then one day I got drunk in the morning and went home like I always did. Same routine, but for some reason, I called up the doc and asked him to get me into treatment. Getting sober meant that I had to ask God to help me, but I think that my family did the asking. I believe in my heart that although they're dead, they know I'm sober. One thing that helped was when I was just getting sober, I saw this program about children with allergies. When you feed some kids milk, they go nuts. So the allergy concept of alcoholism set in immediately. I can see how my mind changed, how my actions changed, how my priorities changed. I believe that God allowed me to listen and see things. With that concept, there is no doubt in my mind: as long as I don't take a drink, I'll be okay.

Nancy

I DID NOTHING IN MY LIFE for so long, because I was doing drugs, that it's important to me not to waste any time. Sometimes I want to just sleep and sleep and sleep, but I can't because I have a production compulsion. And then I get to a point where my body says, "Sorry, you have to go to sleep." When I first found out that I was HIV-positive, in 1986, I decided to shoot as much heroin and cocaine as I could until I died. I did a pretty good job at it until I woke up one day and realized, Shit, I'm still here, and this isn't how I want to spend the rest of my life. I think my will to live was a lot more intense than I had realized. I also think that there were things that I needed to learn before I died, so it wasn't okay for me to just give up and shoot drugs until I die. Because shooting drugs is basically giving up.

IN EARLY sobriety a lot of people think they're going to die, which is kind of funny. It's like they think that they won't be able to deal with the feelings they have. People have so much fear that they don't know how to get past that. Some die before they do. I've lost a lot of friends to both addiction and AIDS. I did this outreach thing at 16th and Mission for women who were junkies and prostitutes, to get them on health care. I was down there thinking how one friend of mine was really brutally murdered—she was a prostitute and someone picked her up and murdered her. I go to these places and have these images of people being really stuck in a spot. So her image was really in my mind when I went there.

I REALLY make distinctions between people who get to resolve their issues and live their lives in a certain way before they die and people who die being addicts without getting that resolved. I've also known people who died of AIDS who never even used and didn't get to resolve their purpose in life. One of the saddest things to see is people die before they're really finished here. It's not like I go, I'm done with my life. I do things. I paint. I teach a class that just started this month. I volunteer at a lot of places. I work at the Center for Living, which is a drop-in center for people with ARC and HIV, and I work for Laurel, which responds to life-threatening diseases, I work for SHANTI. I like my life and I want to live as much of it as I can, but if I died today, it would be okay. But for some people, they never get to a point of feeling okay about their lives.

L. W.

AFTER I'D BEEN SOBER AWHILE, my life improved and I began to put less and less importance on recovery and recovering people. So by the time I left for Paris, I was trying to lead my own life on my own guidelines. I took sobriety for granted. I've always struggled with the issue of giving myself over completely to my recovery. At first, I began to drink coffee. I was in Paris walking around with my bottle of Evian while everyone else was drinking their way to merriment. The pub downstairs from the youth hostel was full of people carousing, drinking, and getting laid—and I was feeling like a geek. I'd been sober five years, and I was twenty-six years old and out of the country for the first time. The first thing I did was to start drinking coffee, then came cigarettes, then sugar. Then I met a woman and we started a trip to Africa by car. I was still in France at that time, but by the time we reached Africa, a joint was going around again. The first few times I said no, and then finally, I said, "Fuck it" and took it. I didn't even get high. I was really disappointed, so I went to the car and got some whiskey. I felt like I had jumped off a cliff into the abyss. I was very curious as to what would happen. And what happened was that I thought about drinking and smoking pot every day.

THAT WAS the end of my first round of recovery. Before I relapsed, I had stopped smoking and drinking coffee, and I was eating really well. I sold my car and bicycled everywhere. I was pretty fanatical about it and self-righteous. Caffeine and nicotine are drugs, and they definitely alter the way you feel. I still drink coffee and wonder about that, but it's an issue that I can't bother with, because it's a tangent—and I love to get sidetracked. It's something that I'd love to change, but it really doesn't matter to me whether anybody else smokes or drinks. It's not a contest anymore. It's not a matter of being more or less sober than other people.

I LEARNED a lot from my relapse. After it was over, I was liberated once again. I was shown at the deepest level of my being that I am an alcoholic and it is not going to go away. And it's much easier to lead a sober life than to try to change who I am. Any doubts that I had that I'm an alcoholic, that it was because I was too young or whatever, were removed. I knew that this was it. Because nothing changed. I would drink every day; it consumed all my thoughts. There's another positive aspect of my having used. It smashed my ego some more, and I needed that. I thought that I was better than some other people.

Traci

I'VE ALWAYS HAD THIS WEIRD RELATIONSHIP with food. Even probably before the drugs. But I guess the problems really started when I went to college. I was only sixteen, and I was so little. I didn't even start to develop physically until I was a sophomore. By the time I finished college, I had grown into a woman and become very conscious of my body. I felt really fat during this whole time and had a nervous breakdown by the time I got out of college. I ended up going to this "fat farm" in North Carolina, where I actually learned how to throw up.

MY FOOD and drugs were so intertwined, it's hard to figure it out sometimes. When I went to the hospital in New York for anorexia, I was also alcoholic and drinking throughout my entire stay. But nobody really focused on that because I was so thin. It was like, anything I could possibly do not to feel. I mean anything. I was a coke addict, but I still binged my ass off. I wasn't even hungry; it had nothing to do with hunger—it had to do with stuffing and having no feelings. I remember one time, I'm driving to Burger King and all I'm thinking about is I've got to get this food in. You know, it's like the drugs and you've got to get your fix. I drive to Burger King, and I go to get my food. When I come back out, my lights are on, my car is running, and my door is wide open. I left my entire car open, not even conscious of what I was doing. You know, when you're in the midst of a binge and a purge it's the same as if you're in an alcoholic or drug-induced blackout.

FOOD ABUSE escalates just like drug addiction. Just as the drug and alcohol abuse got more and more severe, the food got more and more restricted, and the exercise got more and more intense. Maybe at the beginning I was throwing up once a week, but at one point I was throwing up twenty-five times a day. And weighing myself fifty times a day. It gets so bad. Eventually I was locked up in a psychiatric place. They put me in Gracie Square Hospital in New York. And in a sense I wanted to be locked away, because I couldn't take care of myself anymore, which was a terrible thing to figure out. Here I was, supposed to be this great thing, this overachiever college girl, theater major extraordinaire, and all I was was ordinary and sick. I was supposed to be somebody, and all I felt like doing was getting skinnier, and small, small, small, so I could just shrink away.

I AM abstinent from chemicals and alcohol. I am not abstinent from bulimia. I still sometimes medicate with food. It's been easier for me to abstain from drugs and alcohol than the food, because with food I have to deal with it every day. It's a toughie. But it's gotten so I've finally reached a place where I'm ready to take a look at some of that stuff, which in a sense is much deeper than even my chemical addiction, although they were related. And I talk about it a lot, and I have even performed a few pieces about it. I'm a performance artist. That's why I really like doing performance art, because it's funny and sad at the same time. I mean, the human condition is sort of funny, I suppose.

Keith

I'M A COUNSELOR AT A TREATMENT CENTER for chemical dependency. I work with men, many of whom have what I like to call the John Wayne Syndrome: Do everything on your own and never ask for help. I try to help them break through that, so they can seek out and receive the help they need to get and stay sober. Most of these people have been out there for years trying to figure out everything on their own, and look where it's gotten them. There's an old line I heard from someone who had stayed sober successfully for several years. He said, "My mind is like a bad neighborhood; I should never go in there alone." You need help to get and stay sober.

SOMETIMES I'LL get a phone call from someone who is doing really well and they'll say thanks. Having some small part in his success is what keeps this work fulfilling. The most painful part of this work is when people die, when they intentionally or unintentionally overdose. Getting that phone call hurts like hell. Most patients say their drug use filled a void for them. One author I've recently read called alcoholism an imperfect spiritual longing. What he meant is that people start out using chemicals to find a sense of serenity and peace that most of us are looking for. Recovery is about finding serenity and peace from some other source. A lot of people, including myself, call that spirituality—that desire to connect with something larger than ourselves. If you don't

have that connection, my personal opinion is that your chances of staying sober are pretty slim.

METHADONE. I don't have much good to say about methadone programs. You got to love a drug created by Hitler's scientists. Some of these for-profit clinics are making a lot of money by keeping people on methadone. One program I know provides a free week of methadone to any addict who brings in a friend. And methadone is actually harder to kick than heroin. Getting off heroin feels like the worst flu times ten. But methadone is worse. During withdrawal your legs hurt, your bones hurt, your hair hurts. It's uncomfortable to lie down; you're sweating constantly even though you're freezing. And a month later, you're still tweaked because it's still not out of your body.

I'VE BEEN sober almost thirteen years. The light started to come on for me when I watched this man in an American Legion bar—he looked to be in his fifties or sixties—drink this water glass full of booze. He was shaking with the DTs and spilling all over himself, but he just had to have that booze. I remember thinking, "I'll quit if I ever get that bad." About nine months later I was sitting in this bar at, like, ten in the morning, totally hung over, thinking, "All you ever do is get drunk, get stoned, take drugs. This is stupid." You know, you hear about people having moments of clarity in the midst of an alcoholic haze? Well, that's what happened to me.

Del

I WAS CLEAN WHEN I FOUND OUT I WAS POSITIVE, but I knew I was positive even before then because of the people I was with. So I stopped my standard ways of meeting people, which were getting drugs, getting drunk, and taking people home from bars, because I was afraid of passing along the virus. But then I got really lonely and isolated, and my addiction progressed to the point where I wasn't functioning at all. I got too tweaked, too wigged-out to work or do day-to-day tasks.

EVEN AFTER I got sober I never really felt like I fit in, especially in the gay arena. I never felt that I was cute enough. And that kind of affected my decisions about where I went and how I did things. Like in early recovery, I hooked up with one person from my using days, and we became buddies. I hung out with him instead of building a support system. In the third year of my sobriety, I met the person who would become my lover. Then my friend died, and within another four days my lover died. So I was without any support system at all. It was hard not using after they died, but both my friend and my lover died clean. And that is something I would like to do. I knew then that if I used, I would do it to die, not to get high.

THAT'S WHEN I started asking for help, reaching out to people, letting people know me. It's really been a gift. I don't have a lot of real close relationships, though. I just don't have the time. Real relationships take years to develop—to have your fights, your making-up. Besides, most of the people I know are gone. I've gotten to the point since my lover died that I don't want to put anybody through the process of my dying, and I don't want to go through the process again with anybody else who's dying.

THIS WHOLE spiritual thing about having a purpose keeps me going. So many people don't find recovery. I read in this pamphlet that those of us who do find it were chosen to help other people. And that, with my HIV and everything else, has been my belief.

I GUESS I'm ready to move on now. I'm ready to leave this plane, this experience, because I believe that this is just a stop in the overall spiritual thing. Touching, feeling, having a physical body—this is where that happens. Whether it happens again, I don't know. But I'm ready to find out what the next part of this trip is about. Not that I wouldn't like to see Tahiti or become a beach bum in Hawaii, but I've seen and done a lot more than some people get to see and do in their life. And I do know now that love is what we are supposed to experience on this level. I've experienced it, lived with it, and learned to accept it when someone is willing to give it. If that's what this is all about, I've got it.

Hoac

A LONG TIME AGO I was a very angry and mean person. All my life I've been fighting prejudice. So I was very angry. At twelve years old, I considered myself an adult and worked forty hours a week to support my mother and father, and to help get my sisters through school. I figured I was a man because I did what men do, so I started drinking and smoking. In 1966, I married a woman from South Dakota. And through that union I have four children and just celebrated my thirtieth wedding anniversary.

WHEN I got married, I didn't have no spirituality. I am a Degenio Indian from Southern California, but my mother and father were chronic alcoholics. All my life I saw them fight about alcohol. I knew it wasn't right. My wife was Sioux, so I adopted the Lakota way. I said to her, "You're my wife. I love you and you have a strong culture and strong traditions. I want to learn." For twenty-eight years I threw myself into that way of thinking. Nine years ago I got my pipe, and I have helped the medicine man with ceremonies for eight years. I was scared at first because my wife said being a pipe carrier is a hard road. You have got to be humble and be willing to give. And when you think you can't give anymore, you still got to give. You got to give through every aspect of your life—your time, your work, everything. And that fits with what I'm doing now.

I AM senior counselor for American Indian Services in Minneapolis. I am here to give of my knowledge and experiences. I tell people that I'm not a perfect man. If I were perfect, I would be a spirit. But I am a common man—flesh and blood—with the ability to talk about my experiences and how I've overcome them. The people who complete their work here walk away with the sense that they have gained something to pass on to their children. I tell them that they have to want change. Everybody says sobriety is important, but change is also important. And that's one of the hardest things about this work. We can't change the people in this community economically, so we have to help them change spiritually. I help them think through things. I ask them why they say they need to drink when their grandfathers didn't need to drink. I ask them why they make another man rich by buying his liquor. I tell them to stop taking money out of their pockets to set it on the desk of rich men. Put the money to good use instead.

MOST OF the people we see have no idea who they are. When the government took young people off the reservations and put them in boarding schools or foster homes, they were taken away from their teachings and traditions. So they don't have any values to say why something is good or bad. And they don't have a supportive base to run to when they are having problems. We teach them where they have come from; and we teach them spirituality, because they don't know what it is.

I BELIEVE that we are here to learn something, and when we have learned all that we are supposed to learn, we will leave this world, old or young. But I am very fortunate that the spirit in my body is going to be with me for a long time. That's what they tell me in ceremony.

Stevie

THINGS ARE SO DIFFERENT that when I go back home to New Jersey, my old friends don't recognize me. I look different, and I carry myself differently. It's not necessarily how I dress or different hair. It's the fact that my eyes are crystal clear. My consciousness is pretty clear too. Today I can look you in the eye. I'm sincere, I don't have to dodge things or wear long sleeves during the day. I don't have to wear a ton of makeup and pretend that I'm something I'm not. I feel really good about myself and my life, in a way that I never did before, even when I first got clean. It's taken time and been the result of taking actions and being around people who love what they are doing. I was told, If you want what they have, get clean, and you'll have it too. And that's been true.

FOR INCOME, I work on films and music videos. I've been able to go out and find people to teach me how to do it, and it's been wild. I can't believe the things that have happened to me. If you had told me I'd be working and living in a beautiful home, if you had even suggested me not wearing black, if you had told me that I'd be working on some amazing videos in amazing locations, I'd say, "Get out of here!" Who knew? I think I have an idea of what I want out of life, but I've found

that the plans that God has for me supersede the plans I have for myself. God's are the ones that I always wanted but never knew. My greatest gift wasn't getting everything on the Christmas list, it was the thing that I didn't expect, like love. I mean who would have thought that a junkie could walk out in the middle of the day with short sleeves and no sunglasses and have a little coffee with a couple of friends? Those moments are priceless.

THE MOST important thing in my recovery was overcoming the thought that if you stop using or drinking, you're a loser: You'll have to have a nine-to-five job, and life will be reduced to gray. I thought, I'll never fly again. But when I got clean, I was given wings. That's when I really began to live a life that I could hold on to with both hands. There's that old belief that drugs and alcohol gave me something, that I couldn't perform unless I was loaded. It's a lie. There's probably nothing that I can't do if I don't want to. There are people around me who are willing to help me and guide me, and I'm willing to listen. I didn't have that luxury when I was using. You can't conduct life from the bathroom floor. You can't do it from the closet of your bedroom. And I was there for many hours and days.

Andrew

I KNEW IT TEN YEARS AGO. I had so many friends who went before me. I knew that I was an alcoholic. I just thought I could go overtime, I could beat it, I'd turn the corner and the right relationship would solve my problem, the right situation at work would solve my problem. I thought, well, I can handle almost anything. Crises: bus full of nuns overturns on the highway, I'm out there in a T-shirt in the middle of winter, and I know what to do; the *Titanic* is sinking, and I know how to prevent it; you're having a crisis in your life, and I know just how to solve it. But if it involves romance or finance, I am a helpless little salmon thrashing around in the banks of the street while this big bear is coming down on me. That's exactly what it was like. I kept trying to get sober for the sake of my friends who were concerned. For my parents, but not for me. I was exposed to recovery, but I never admitted to myself that I was out of control.

WOODY ALLEN once said, "Ninety-nine percent of life is just showing up." I never did that. I never showed up. The most important thing that I've learned about life when I got sober was how great it is. Yes, some nights I want to tear my hair out, I want to sit and cry. That's not the fun part. But you have to have that. The good is going to come with the bad. I always thought that what I was doing was a panacea for all my ills. I thought that it was easier than showing up for life with my helmet and my pads. Eventually, we do all those things that we do to get outside of ourselves—sex, drugs, alcohol—and the most important thing that we can do is just endure the first day, put on the pads, and go on out there, because life is worth living.

I'M A chef at Café Un Deux Trois in Minneapolis. They say that the toughest place to apply the principles of sobriety is at work. I wish that I was a good enough human being to treat the people I work with everyday the way you treat the little old ladies on the bus. That's a great goal. I'm a maniacal, ego-driven success freak. I want success here and now, but that's not how life works. So I just keep trying to do the best job that I can every day and hope that somebody notices. And if nobody notices, I can still go to bed at night knowing that I did everything I could.

THIS IS the only disease with a mental component that tells you that you don't have a disease. If you told every leukemia victim in this country that there is a cure, all you have to do is follow some simple directions and you won't die, 100 percent of them would do it. Tell that to alcoholics, and perhaps 15 percent would. That's a very scary thing to me. That's why I take recovery very seriously. I've had too many friends who ended up hanging themselves or driving the wrong way down the highway, or just disappeared off the face of the earth. It's life and death. There's no time for that kind of bullshit. Either you want it or you don't, and if you do, let's go. Pedal to the metal because you can't half-measure recovery. You just can't.

Cecilia

I WAS MARRIED BY THE TIME I was eighteen, and it was an abusive relationship. We were both using and I got pregnant, so I stopped using for that time when I was pregnant, and he kept using. I had the baby, and we ended up getting divorced when the baby was three months old—just an itty-bitty little baby, and it was really sad. But after we were divorced, probably just half a year later, I started using again. Then when the baby was maybe eighteen or twenty months old, one day the house caught fire. I didn't set the house on fire. It just caught on fire, and I just sat there holding the baby and waiting for us to burn to death, thinking that it would be better for both of us if it just ended now, and feeling very relieved. Then a voice in me said, "No, you can't do this to the baby." So I took him out. They put the fire out and everybody lived, but then I knew that I needed to do something so that I could take care of that baby until he was, like, twelve, and then I'd be okay—and he could take care of himself, and I could use, and I wouldn't hurt him.

ON THE break-room table at work there was this magazine that told about a bunch of people that had recovered from alcoholism. It was an old, old magazine, and I don't know why it was lying there, but I read it. It talked about this lady involved with recovery. I called her that day, and I stopped using. But I only stopped using for a short time. I picked up again, saying, "I'm an alcoholic, so I can still smoke some weed." That went on for about a year, me thinking, "I'm a drug addict—no, I'm an alcoholic." Then after about a year, this lady called and said, "You know, you've been clean a year." And I said, "Oh, man, I haven't been clean a year!" But I said I'll earn it, and I haven't used since then. That was back in 1983.

YOU KNOW, I can appreciate things more. Life is so exciting; you wake up in the morning and you just want to see what happens next. And there's never a dull moment. I never have to go searching for something to do or someone to play with. I think sobriety progresses and happens in stages, just like the disease does. And in early sobriety, people get out there and they're searching for help and they're getting involved in the sober community, and that's really an exciting time. Then after a while, you would tend to get complacent and you would think, "Well, I haven't picked up in a long time, and all these people just have the same old things to say and they're getting really boring." And that's such a dangerous time, because you get bored. You don't appreciate things if you're bored, if you don't broaden your understanding and keep searching. If you work past that, it gets exciting all over again.

NOW I just feel happy. If I felt that life was going to end today, I would not regret the way that I have lived, but at the same time I would feel like I was missing out on something. There's so much that I want to do, so much I want to see. And I have so much fun. A teacher told me a long time ago that only one in ten people will live through this disease, and you need to remember the one. I remember him telling me that, "You live for the one that makes it."

Hal

I'M MARRIED NOW. I married a professional woman. She's a suit person, an attorney. Being in a relationship had always been incredibly important to me because I had done some things in my addiction that I'm ashamed of. Not so much the actions but the feelings behind it. I sold myself to men, and sometimes I enjoyed it. Sometimes I felt as if I was being loved. So my head started telling me that I was gay. For the first seven years of my recovery, I was in a relationship whether I wanted to be or not. I was in it because that meant I was okay and that meant I wasn't gay. I could also just pretend that some of the past stuff had never happened. But after seven years, I exploded. It was just after I bought this house and I was with this one particular lady, and our relationship progressed to where we were so angry with each other that she slapped me a couple of times and I slapped her back. And that was one thing I never wanted to do in recovery. That's one thing I told myself that I would never have to do again was to hit a woman, because I had done that before in my addiction and I always felt small when I did that. Anyway, I lashed out and slapped her. Whether it was justified, whether I felt she deserved it, that's immaterial. I sat here for two weeks crying.

I HAVE this beautiful home, I have this business, money, all this materialistic stuff, and yet I'm miserable. I went back into therapy, to a woman I had seen five years prior to that, and I went back and started crying. Just sobbing, snot coming out of my nose, I felt about that high. And she sat across from me smiling and happy and said, "I've been waiting for you to come back." It was time for me to deal with some more issues. And one of them was the feelings behind the action. And once that came up and came out, I didn't even date for four or five months. And I really enjoyed not having to be in a relationship. And it's not that I was gay, but it was that I thought I might be, and never talked about it. That was a start to being with women I really wanted. I always took women who were younger than me, that made less money than me, and women that I also thought I could control. My wife now, I could not control her; I don't want to. It's been the first relationship that I've been in for more than a year, and there hasn't even been an argument. I tell other people that and they say that's abnormal, and I say, "No it's not, it's different. I've never experienced it, but it's not abnormal." But I had to cross over and deal with my own stuff before I could go on and have this woman in my life.

Kathy

ONE THING THAT I USED TO SAY when I was out getting drunk or high with my friends was "Why am I doing this to myself?" And they would say, "Sure, Kathy, have another drink. Have another line." Those were times when I was sincere. And I still didn't get it. I was losing good jobs. My priorities were getting high and drinking. That was more important than myself or my spirituality. The funny thing is that, even then, I still had a higher power. I knew that I had something watching over me that was letting me experience what I was experiencing, but that it would eventually get to a point where everything's going to crash. And that's when it would all start anew. But I didn't know how or when. I didn't know whether that would be me still living, beginning a new life without the handcuffs of drugs and alcohol. Or was it going to eliminate my life on earth and begin another life. I told my friends. I knew it was going to happen. Sometimes, even when you're using, clarity does hit. If you are even a smidgen awake, you are going to hear it. That's what started happening to me—I realized, This is what is destroying me. Before, I thought it was everything else—circumstances, economics, people, places, things.

BUT WHEN I finally left it up to my higher power, I found that there is nothing that Kathy cannot do today. I'm going to a school that I've wanted to go to my whole life. I gave God my soul, my will, my dreams, my everything, to get me out of that hellhole that I was in, and He gave me back my life. That to me is the most important thing. That is what keeps me going. Nothing more, nothing less. Material things aren't going to give me the spiritual satisfaction that I need. I've had all these things, and all they did is make me buy more drugs.

MY SISTER says that when I was using, she never wanted to be near me and was ashamed of me. My mother felt the same way. My friends slowly and surely stopped associating with me. But since I've been in sobriety, all they do is look at me in wonder and say, "We don't know who this person is." Sometimes I don't know either, but that's the real Kathy, that's the real me who has been hiding for so long. Just hearing that from my family and friends, I know that there is growth going on. I was so selfish for so long. It was always "I" and "me." In some ways, I guess, I still am. But with the help of other people, I'm learning to say "us, we, you."

Michelle

MENTALLY AND PHYSICALLY I think I stopped being able to handle the drug like I used to. I had this uncontrollable movement—this constant rocking—that people who do a lot of speed have. I call it "doing the tuna." And I was soaking-wet sweaty often. It was embarrassing, because people would look at me. I lost my composure. I remember one time during a drug raid, a cop walked passed the chair I was in—I had done a little too much dope—and I literally sat upside down in the chair. They say that with speed you don't die from an overdose, you just go crazy. I was aware that I was slipping in and out of reality, that I was losing my mind.

DURING ONE amphetamine psychosis, I was on the roof of a seven-story building, ready to jump. I was hallucinating that I was being chased by my husband and that he was trying to kill me. Maybe God saved me, but suddenly my mind came back and I realized that I was hallucinating. I turned around and walked right off that roof. I had never been in such a bad state before. But I knew at that point that I was done; that was it. That's why I stopped using; it wasn't any fun anymore. It just wasn't working. A straight friend of mine was working in a treatment program and said to give him a call when I was ready. And I knew that I was ready. I drank that weekend, partied really hard, came back, and got into recovery. I have been sober now for three and a half years.

I FOUND out I was HIV-positive during my second treatment, and I relapsed as a result. I have since learned that denial can be a real killer in drug addiction, but denial is almost necessary for dealing with HIV. There are some days when you just do not need to deal with it. Because it will kill you, literally, to think about it daily. With my addiction, I have the comfort of knowing that I'll be okay if I stay clean. But my HIV is showing in little ways, and it's obvious that it's going to be the end of me unless they come up with a cure. Sometimes I welcome it. I don't want to sound depressing, but when I realized I was positive, I knew, well, that there must be something more to this life.

THAT'S WHY I am working on my spirituality in sobriety. I want to be a better, more spiritual person. I kind of have a traditional God-as-the-old-guy-with-the-white-beard view of God. A comforting, loving, paternal sort of God really works for me. That's what I need. And so I'm looking back at Catholicism, which is my faith. My family is very spiritual, and they have all welcomed me back. My mother's love has enveloped me at times. She is the most loving, caring person I know. Knowing that she is there has given me the strength to continue. She's a nurse and I always feel safe in her arms.

Del

WHEN I STARTED RECOVERY, I was very hostile and angry at everyone. Everyone avoided me because I had a drumbeat of anger going through me. But over the years, through the recovery process, I feel that, today, when I'm around people, instead of wanting to punch them, my tendency is to give them a hug. It's like the difference between day and night. I'm not jealous or envious of people as I used to be. And I'm not as lonely as I used to be, even at this point where I'm not in a relationship. I don't feel lonely or as if I've been cheated. Being in recovery as long as I have, you have to keep finding new tools and reinvent yourself and keep growing. As long as you are sober, you have to keep finding new ways. At that fifteen-year juncture, I was not a happy camper and—just for me—I developed a personal relationship with Christ, and that has given me a totally new perspective. It was almost like starting over. And that connection enabled me not to be jealous of other people.

RECOVERY IS not a religious program. We're encouraged to find a higher power, because what goes along with this disease is this belief that we're God, almost. Most addicts live their lives as if they were God. The key is to find a power that works for you. And the more personal it is, the better it is. It doesn't make any difference who you select, as long as it works for you. I just discovered recently that I have such a need to acknowledge my higher power by name because it gives me a burst of courage every time I mention His name. Even after this length of time, I still have a lot of fears. When you've been sober awhile, you become more in touch with your feelings than you do in early sobriety. And so you need a higher power. Not that you don't need one at any stage, but you never outgrow the basic need.

EVERYBODY HAS to deal with their feelings, in or out of recovery. But my feeling is that the alcoholic is like everybody else, only more so. If a non-addict is a little fearful, I'm going to be in terror. If they're a little happy, I'm going to be delirious. Also, I came out of a violent home where there was alcoholism and I didn't feel safe. That set in motion a fear-based and shame-based life. I don't say this with any regret—I'm grateful to have a recovery program to deal with it. In fact, I'm grateful that I'm an alcoholic, because if I wasn't, I would have had a much narrower outlook on life. I wouldn't have taken the risks that I did, and I certainly wouldn't have as close a connection with my higher power today. So I'm a richer person spiritually and emotionally than I would have been if I had not had this affliction. That is a gut belief.

Jim

THE BIGGEST PART ABOUT USING was being a real man. If I was a real man, then I was the best at everything. I could drink more than anyone else and make it through all that and it didn't affect me. I was excellent at drinking a bottle of whiskey and still being able to drive and talk to cops, and shit like that. To me that meant I was a man; and if I fucked a lot of women, I was a man. And I think it's because I always had a superman in mind who was judging me all the time. I think that's the main thing that you are going to find through all of it. My recovery has nothing to do with finding new places to be a man. It has to do with the integrity of people and my work with relationships.

MY DAD was sort of a John Wayne–type figure. My mom stayed home and raised the children and he was the man. That made me grow up believing that women stayed home and took care of the children, and the men worked and took care of everything, almost in a mystical sort of way. I grew up thinking, To be a real man, you gotta be able to crack the safe and rise above the occasion and be superhuman and take care of women. And I think when you all of a sudden are in your teens, those become pressures and not just lofty ideals. Being able to score points in the last minutes of the game and all that.

I GOT sober at just the right moment. There's a guy in a story who says that life is about inches and seconds. I came to a recovery group at the precise hour, the precise day, to hear what I needed to hear to get me to come the next day. Whereas if I had waited a few more minutes or a few more hours, it wouldn't have happened. So people just have to be ready to hear these things, and they have to do all the work. I think I found out that you have to do all the work. Alcoholics won't accept help until they're ready to do it.

AS FAR as achieving things, I want to be successful at whatever I do, but I haven't found an occupation I love. I'm a salesman, a businessman. To me it doesn't matter what I'm selling, it's that I'm in a working relationship and selling stuff. I like building those kinds of relationships, people trusting you and bringing you something. I'm a good salesman, but I don't love it. Money isn't a big object—as hard as I'm gonna work is as much as I'm gonna get.

I WOULD like to be madly in love with someone, have a true relationship with someone. If it's not that, I don't want a relationship. It's either extreme—I want the princess bride or I don't want anything. I think that's a big goal. If that doesn't happen, I don't want to have a mediocre relationship with someone that I care about—I just want to keep following my heart. I just want to keep following what I am, letting things happen. And if I stay on the path that's right for me and using certain principles, that will lead me to a good place. I don't want to navigate the river only because I know that sixty miles down there's a town that I'm going to go to. I just want to go with the flow of the river, Eastern philosophy–wise, wherever it takes me. I can see myself in the Peace Corps, if that's the right thing to do.

Yvette

I THINK THE FIRST THING I SAW when I got sober was that I was sad and unhappy, and had been sad and unhappy for a long time. I think I was unhappy since I was a child. I remember hanging out the window just to get attention, wishing that a neighbor would drive by and call my parents to say, "Yvette is hanging out the window." It's not like I came from a broken home or that we were poor and in a violent neighborhood. I came from a very comfortable home, and my parents have been married for forty-one years.

I REMEMBER smoking crack in my parent's basement at, like, three in the morning. I heard something. It was probably just the wind, but I thought someone was trying to break into the house. The crack had me tweaked and paranoid. I called 911, and the cops came to the house with their guns drawn. Then my father came downstairs to ask if I was okay, and I was so embarrassed. I could see the disappointment in his eyes. But I still wanted him to go away so I could finish smoking. I guess that's when I hit bottom, when I saw that I was completely alienated from my family.

MY CHANGE really began when I got into a support group for black women who had been users. That's when I really got it. Until then I had abstained from alcohol and other drugs, but when I had sex it wasn't safe. I still didn't think enough of myself to protect my body. I didn't think enough of myself to feel angry or disappointed. Being with these women has given me a place to talk about my life and be heard. I've been working on trying to get my body back. There's a part of me that's been out of my body for the last three years. When I stopped doing drugs, I picked up on food.

BECAUSE OF the work that I do—a lot of my clients are African-American and they're in the hospital—I trace their sickness up until they die. So I've gone through some powerful life experiences. What is great is that I've picked up photography in the last few months and just photographing my clients, sort of like documenting the epidemic. I don't know what I'm going to do from here on. I just have to remember that I can keep on living. There was a point where I was just coming home, getting a pint of ice cream, a diet Pepsi, and I was in bed at 5:30. I went to my doctor and asked for some antidepressants, and that didn't help. I was just sad. And it made sense for me to be sad. I've been with this organization for four years now. And it has given me a place to do my own advocacy for my own life and do work for my community.

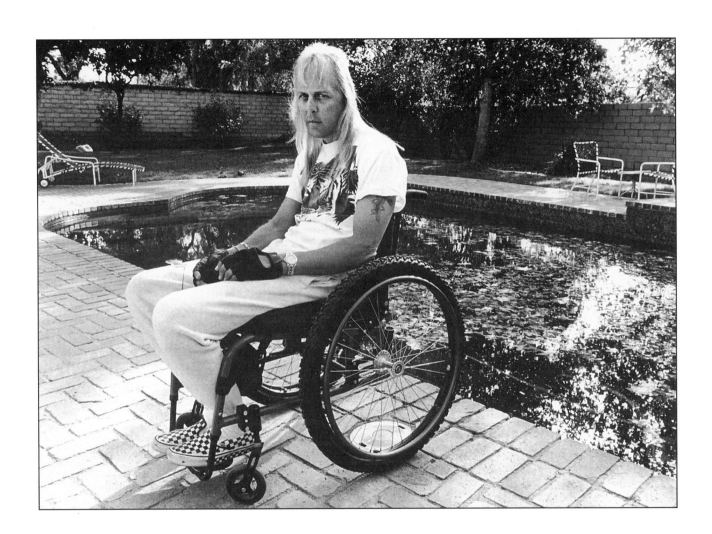

Rollandrock

I'M A PRESIDENT of a California nonprofit corporation. I go to high schools and talk about drinking and using and the way it took my life. In the last five years I've spoken in front of almost a half a million high school students, mostly in California and Hawaii. The response from them has been incredible. One time I got home and my post office box had 600 letters in it. I just looked at them and thought, Look at that, I made a difference! I never made a difference in anybody's life, let alone my own. I always was the screwup. I did whatever I wanted, but eventually, I had to pay the price.

BEING IN a wheelchair for almost seventeen years wasn't what I wanted. But because a friend and I got into a car that neither one of us had any business being in, we got into a nasty accident, and I broke my neck. Now I've got to deal with that. The way that I dealt with it before was with drugs and alcohol. I never wanted to feel the way that I did, like an outcast or like I didn't belong. I acted like some kind of a maniac, like a comet on fire. I thought they'd at least understand that I was crazy. I don't know how I got from there to "Don't drink no matter what." Sometimes when life gets serious and real, and I don't like it, I get angry that I can't get out that bottle of tequila and start feeling better. But if I were to go drink now, it'd be total torment. I was sober one other time, and I didn't know in my gut that I was an alcoholic and an addict, so I relapsed for ten years. I don't want that again.

WHY DO I talk to these kids in school? Because I found myself living a lifestyle that I discovered was very serious and deadly. I found out that my chemical dependency was a symptom of a deeper problem—but I didn't have a choice anymore. I had to use. I never had anybody tell me that drinking and using and acting like an animal would make me miserable and lonely. All I got in elementary school was a sign that said SPEED KILLS. But nobody really told me what would happen. Okay, I'll go to prison, or I'll be dead, or my parents will beat the hell out me. I can handle all that. What they couldn't tell me was how I would feel about myself and about other people. I treated myself like shit, but I don't anymore. I let the kids know that there's a loneliness to be found in a bottle that can't be explained. It's the kind of loneliness that is accompanied by thoughts of suicide and total desperation. I was lucky that I never followed through with any of that. I had a gun in my mouth, and I'm really glad I didn't pull the trigger. The next day I got sober, and I've been clean ever since.

Jennifer

I WAS IN A MARRIAGE where, as I was walking down the aisle, I knew right away it wasn't right. And right away I wanted out. I felt smothered, so I would come home and drink beer. I had stopped doing Valium and cocaine years earlier, but I started drinking beer because someone had told me that you couldn't get addicted to it. I was drinking twelve beers a day, often all alone in my backyard. There was a mirror in the hallway I had to pass on my way out to the backyard, and I remember feeling very scared after looking in it because my face had become so gray. I felt so ashamed sitting back there, wondering why I hadn't done anything with my life.

THEN I met Roland, my present husband, while delivering pet supplies to his house. There was a connection right away, and something mystical and spiritual about him. He was able to communicate such a sense of peace and serenity. I immediately felt comfortable. At his house I was with him for what seemed like five minutes, but we had actually talked for more than two hours. Before I left, we traded telephone numbers, and I asked what he was doing that night. He said he was speaking at a recovery group. I went home and told my husband that I wanted to go to a recovery group. He thought they were for crazy people and didn't want me to go. But I felt compelled. I was drawn, so I got into my car to go. I ended up sitting in my car for a couple

of hours, though. I just couldn't force myself to get out. I scribbled a note to Roland, and we met a couple of days later for lunch. That was when he told me he was a recovering alcoholic. He inspired me to get clean. We could talk for hours, and I thought that was beautiful.

I FEEL like God sent Roland to me. I moved in with him, quit my job, got sober, and left my husband. And because I did those things, I was able to go to school and become a dental assistant and buy a horse. And then it dawned on me that there must be a God, because I remember sitting alone drinking in my backyard, feeling compelled to get sober by three wishes: I wanted to become a dental assistant, own a horse, and go to the African Zoo to see all the wild animals.

NEARLY EVERYONE on my father's side has died because of drinking. My uncle, who was more my father than my real father, knew this and used to call me to check whether I was drinking. I would always lie and tell him I wasn't drinking. I'm only the third one to get sober—me, my uncle, and my grandfather. I feel special about that because my grandfather was in one of the first recovery groups in Akron, Ohio, in 1941. A museum there commemorates the group and mentions my grandfather. He helped a lot of people, inspired them to get clean. I wish he could see me now.

Acknowledgments

This book was made possible with the help of Christi Atkinson, who helped get this project off the ground; my agent, Susan Golomb; my editor, Marie Timell; and my publisher, Michael Fragnito.

I offer special thanks to the people who offered their support:

CALIFORNIA	FLORIDA	GEORGIA	MINNESOTA	NEW YORK
JUSTINE KERNER	JUDI CORDO	CAMERON FROSTBAUM	TOM SANN	KATE LEHMAN
BONNIE DALEY	IRIS MALDONADO		GREG MARTIN	MACALL POLAY
MARY LINGERFELT	JAMES SEABARKROB		MARC CARDEN	JOHN SANN
DONNA SPROULL	TIA PALMISANO		ELENA SOHMER	KARYN KUHL
NICKI DEWER			TERRY MARTIN	KATHLEEN CAMPELL
NANCY LeMOINS			PHOEBE PETTERSON	UNCLE ALAN
CATHERINE BUDH-RAJA			KEITH JENSEN	TRACY HESTON
SUSAN JENNINGS			PAIGE MANGER	BETH TITTLE
			DONNA JANSON	DARLYNE BAUGH
			JUDY HANSON	JAMES APT
			JODI RAJCICH	JAIME CERTILMAN

I would also like to thank the people who were photographed and not included in the final selection:

CALIFORNIA		FLORIDA		MINNESOTA		NEW YORK	
DWAYNE	STEPHANIE	JUDI	ANDREA	ERIC	TIM	ADDISON	ROBIN
RON	LISA	JAMES	DONALD	COLLEEN	CLAUDE	ANNE	CECILY
ROBERT	ERIC	SUSAN	RENÉ	ANNA	BRIDGET	DAVID	JONN
RICHARD	TIEN	GARY	LESLEY	JODI	GERALDA	NIC	STEVEN
KIRK	LEAH	MICHAEL	KATHLEEN	HUNTER	MORGAN	JUDY	TRACY
ARTHUR	BILL			ANGELA	RON	CRAIG	BRYAN
				JACK	ANDREW	CHRIS	
				STEPHEN	MICHAEL		
				HENRY	BARY		
				RITU	DALE		
				JONI			

I am grateful to David Ford, who helped edit the interview transcriptions, and to Angelica Fenner and Josh Blatter for transcribing the interviews.

ADAM GAYNOR holds a B.S. degree in special education, and has done graduate photography study at the International Center of Photography in New York. He divides his time between teaching photography to learning-disabled children and his portrait work. Mr. Gaynor's work has a distinct emotional content. His experiences in his own recovery inspired him to create the portraits in this book. He shoots with Leica Cameras and Kodak Tri-X film, and prints on Ilford paper. He currently lives in New York City.

TERENCE T. GORSKI, M.A., NCAC II, a noted expert on addiction, is an internationally acclaimed pioneer in relapse prevention therapy. He is the president of CENAPS Corporation, a private organization that offers professional training and consulting in relapse prevention treatment. Mr. Gorski has more than twenty years' experience as a therapist, supervisor, program administrator, and consultant on recovery and relapse prevention. He is the author or co-author of numerous articles and many well-received books published worldwide. These include: *Learning to Live Again: A Guide for Recovery from Alcoholism, Family Recovery—Growing Beyond Addiction, Counseling for Relapse Prevention, Passages Through Recovery: An Action Plan for Preventing Relapse,* and *Staying Sober: A Guide for Relapse Prevention.*

If you are in need of assistance, please call
the National Drug and Alcohol Treatment Hotline:

(800) 662-4357

That's (800) 662-HELP

Remember that it is never too late to ask for help.

Please note that the Center for Substance Abuse Treatment (CSAT) and any of the organizations referred to in the hot line are not affiliated in any way with this book, although CSAT kindly gave its permission for the hot line to be published here.